DATE DUE

APR 1 9 2004		
JUN 2 9 2004		
JUL 2 3 2004		

D O

*N*OREEN *O*LSON

Foreword by WILL FERGUSON

THE SCHOOL BUS

DOESN'T STOP HERE
ANY MORE

LIFE AND TIMES
ON A *Rural Route*

Douglas & McIntyre
VANCOUVER/TORONTO

Douglas & McIntyre Ltd.
2323 Quebec Street, Suite 201
Vancouver, British Columbia
Canada v5t 4s7
www.douglas-mcintyre.com

National Library of Canada Cataloguing in Publication
Olson, Noreen
The school bus doesn't stop here any more:
life and times on a rural route / by Noreen Olson.
Selections from 6 previously published books
plus new material. Essays originally published in her
biweekly column for the *Didsbury Review*.

ISBN 1-55365-029-8

1. Olson, Noreen—Family—Anecdotes.
2. Farm life—Alberta—Anecdotes. I. Title.
PS8579.L76A16 2004   C818'.5402   C2003-907176-6

Early versions of some of these stories appeared
in the *Didsbury Review* and in
The Kitchen Table Collection, Books One through Six.

Editing by Mary Schendlinger
Cover illustration from Mary Evans Picture Library
Cover and text design by Jessica Sullivan
Printed and bound in Canada by Friesens
Printed on acid-free paper

We gratefully acknowledge the financial support
of the Canada Council for the Arts, the British Columbia Arts Council,
and the Government of Canada through the Book Publishing Industry
Development Program (BPIDP) for our publishing activities.

For my husband Ralph Olson—
best beloved, best friend and source of some of my best lines.

CONTENTS

Foreword *xi*

WINTER *135*

FOREWORD

"The more I write about the street I live on, the more I write about the world."—MICHEL TREMBLAY

I was living in southern Japan, lost in the haze of a tropical heat wave amid the trills of cicadas and the impending threat of typhoons, when I first met Noreen Olson. I met Noreen through her writing, in articles clipped from a newspaper in southern Alberta and mailed to her daughter, Kirsten, who was teaching English in a city not far from mine.

Kirsten and I would often get together at the end of the work week to vent our frustrations and revel in our fortune. Japan was good to us, we knew that, but even as we plotted elaborate post-Japan travel routes (Kirsten would see her plans through, hopscotching across Asia and Europe), we realized that our time abroad was only a detour, a fascinating series of side trips that would ultimately have to end. At some point, all journeys lead homeward. Kirsten and I talked about what we had left behind in Canada and what each of us would be returning to. I would tell her horror stories about my days as a struggling film student in Toronto and she, in turn, would regale me with tales about growing up on a farm in the foothills of Alberta.

"You know, my mom writes a column for the paper back home," she said. "You might enjoy it."

And so, one night, after walking Kirsten to the train station down streets lined with steaming noodle shops and tattered paper lanterns, I returned to my apartment with a selection of Noreen Olson's writings. The effect was immediate, like a drink of cool water. Kirsten's mom had a voice that was as clear and clean as a springtime chinook. One of my favourite pieces was "Running the Combine," a small comedic gem that was funny and disarming in just the right ways.

The key to any good writing is finding the universal within the particular, and Noreen Olson does that in spades—literally. She digs a lot of earth in her writing and plants a lot of seeds. She writes about family and friendship, about growing up and growing older. She writes about the changing of the seasons and the passage of time, about life's small triumphs and quirky little lessons.

Snowboarding calves; last-minute science projects; an irrepressible exchange student who wants to cook "shoe cream"; dinners that go wrong and roads that turn treacherous; cattle dogs afraid of hot-air balloons and cats who arrive via air mail: Noreen deals with each of these things as they arise, with a generosity of spirit and no small amount of aplomb. (Frazzled aplomb, but aplomb nonetheless.) Her husband, Ralph, provides some of the best moments, as do their three children, Mark, John and Kirsten. There is a clarity and an honesty in Noreen's writing; she is an author completely devoid of pretension. Would that there were more like her.

When Scott McIntyre, a publisher with a passion for promoting distinctly Canadian voices, asked me which writers I felt deserved a wider audience, I didn't hesitate in naming Noreen Olson. Scott shared my enthusiasm for her work, and I am pleased to provide a foreword for this collection, to help "introduce Noreen to newer readers." Though, really, the only introduction Noreen needs is a comfortable chair, a glowing lamp and a quiet evening of reading.

Gardens figure largely in this book, as do the seasonal cycles of planting and harvest, birth and death, spring and winter. Even the book's title echoes with a sense of time moving by. There is much playfulness here, to be sure, but there is also a tinge of wistfulness, a poignancy that runs just below the surface of so much of what Noreen writes. As a father now myself, I too am watching my young children grow up before my eyes. Like parents everywhere, I am already preparing for the day that the school bus—metaphorically—will pass by our house without stopping as well.

My wife, Terumi, and I moved to Calgary when our first child, Alex, was a toddler, and we were quickly invited "out to the farm." The Olson property is north of Cremona and west of Didsbury, with hilltop views of the Rocky Mountains. Exhilarated by the open space and clean air, Alex ran and ran and ran. He helped pick potatoes and he visited the barn cats and he climbed the fence to watch the cattle. We have been back many times since then, and our visits are always joyous. The meals are enormous, the summer twilights long and languid, and the conversations interlaced with laughter.

Two things stand out at the Olson farm:

In front of the family home sits a sunken grotto, its stone walls entwined with vines and ringed with flowerpots. It looks almost like a miniature quarry. This was the foundation of the original homestead, Noreen explained, built by Ralph's parents when they first broke the land. It was the house that Ralph was born in.

Beyond the grotto, the front yard leads to a field, and in the field sits a glacial erratic: a massive boulder embedded in the earth. Several generations of kids have clambered over this landmark, and a plaque attached to it reads: "In memory of John Olson & Anna Olson . . . who cleared and tilled this land. Dedicated with love and appreciation by their children and grandchildren."

At times, I like to think that the core of who we are—our family, our homes, our history—is an immovable boulder, impervious to rain and snow and the shifting patterns of weather. The light touch of Noreen Olson's writing belies the bedrock beneath. These are stories to enjoy and share like a fistful of dandelions, like coffee at the kitchen table.

Will Ferguson

SPRING

The Christmas tree is hardly down when I take inventory of the seed supply and wonder if the ones that I harvested from our garden will grow. And why did I take so many? I have enough poppy seeds to plant a row from here to Calgary and if all the Gazanias sprout we will have to rent another quarter section.

Seed catalogues arrive in January and I pore over them, and plan. By February I am snipping slips from geraniums and planting tomatoes in flats. In early March a migrating bald eagle, regal as a pharaoh, drops into the big trees east of the corrals and allows us to pay him homage. The first calf arrives on about March 10, and mountain bluebirds begin inspecting our nest boxes on about March 12. As soon as a patch of grass clears under the apple trees, robins start listening for worms, and as soon as a patch of earth shows in a flower bed, I start looking for Trollius, tulips, daffodils and squills.

Spring is erratic in Alberta. It is not unusual to get two feet of snow in early May, but the sun is strong and the snow goes quickly. Our little creek bubbles happily through the greening pasture, steam rises from black garden earth, dandelions pop up overnight and baby calves gambol in the sunshine. This close to the foothills it can freeze again at any time, but by about May 20 all the garden is planted and the lanky, three-foot tomatoes, which I started way too soon, are in the greenhouse and looking limp but hopeful.

Springtime in Alberta, and it's only twelve weeks till fall!

A ᴮEVY OF BIRDHOUSES

ON AN EARLY mid-April morning I was driving down our long, tree-lined lane when a piece of sky broke off, tumbled earthward and caught on the barbed-wire fence. I was so bemused that I narrowly missed the mailbox and turned right instead of left at the gate. I was halfway to Carstairs before I remembered that I was going to a conference near Olds.

"Can we please build some bluebird houses?" I asked my husband Ralph. "I have had the instructions for about five years and now that I have seen a bluebird on the place we really must put up some boxes."

"There is a good piece of half-inch plywood in the machine shed," he told me. "You measure and mark and I'll cut them out and help you nail them together."

My instructions came from Doug Gilroy's Prairie Wildlife column and from an article by Blake Stillings. Mr. Stillings has put up more than 300 bluebird houses on roads northwest of Calgary. In 1981 he had 83 bluebird nests with over 400 young. He also had 153 pairs of tree swallows, 2 pairs of wrens and 3 pairs of chickadees. He says bluebirds prefer to nest in mature deciduous trees with woodpecker holes, but because of land clearing and tough, aggressive starlings (who also like to nest in holes) the bluebirds are hard pressed to find a suitable home.

Gilroy and Stillings gave slightly different measurements for their houses so I compromised at a 9 × 6 floor, probably too big, and a front wall 10 inches high, because Stillings says the 1½ inch hole is cut three inches from the top and Gilroy says to cut it six inches above the floor. The 1½ inch hole admits bluebirds and swallows but not starlings. The inside front wall should be scuffed so that the bird can get a toehold and is not trapped. Don't add a perch—bluebirds don't need it and it gives sparrows a place to sit while they harass the tenants.

It was such a nice big piece of plywood that I decided to make two birdhouses. I found a ruler and a pencil and began. I marked two 9 × 6 floors and eight 6 × 10 walls. I was about to mark the roofs when Ralph arrived.

"Your side walls have to be deeper than your fronts and backs," he said kindly. "You're not dealing with a square floor."

I scribbled out some lines and made new measurements. I accidentally scribbled out one line that I shouldn't have and tried to think of a code that would mean "ignore this scribble". There is no logical way to scribble out a scribble. I turned the plywood over and began again. Two 9 × 6 floors, four 6 × 10 fronts and backs and four 9 × 10 side walls.

My husband was back. "Dear sweet wife," he said patiently, "the side walls have to be wider than the floor in order to overlap the end walls and give me something to nail to."

"Why didn't you tell me that before?" I asked testily. "If you were making a cake I would offer you some help before you messed up twice."

"You have made about two thousand cakes for each of my birdhouses," he replied, reasonable as usual. "And don't turn the plywood over again, it has only two sides."

I scribbled out the offending lines and remeasured 10 × 10 walls. I cannot explain my reasoning but I marked out eight of these 10 × 10 walls, and this time my husband failed to catch the error. When the power saw stopped and the sawdust settled I had four extra side walls and two 9 × 6 roofs, which of course were the same size as the floor but should have been larger to allow for nailing.

Now we had the best part of four roofless birdhouses. My talents obviously do not lie in the construction business. Before things got any worse, Ralph took over and drew four 7 × 10½ inch roofs and four more 6 × 10 fronts and backs. This would make four birdhouses when I had really expected only one.

Three days later some dear friends, Kirsten and Kaare Snarud, gave me two more. Boy, do we have birdhouses, and I treasure every one. Several of them are visible from the house and to check the others I often walk down the lane. The bluebirds are still here, nesting in two boxes. Swallows are nesting in one of Mr. Snarud's houses and two of ours. I am delighted with the whole enterprise but I don't plan a career in architecture.

SAVING THE PREEMIE CALF

ONE MONDAY NIGHT when the yearlings came in for chop, one little heifer stayed behind. Ralph went out to check on her and her problem was pitifully clear—two tiny hooves extended from the birth canal and the rest of the baby would not be coming unassisted.

"I'll need a little help here," he told us. "A yearling is having a calf."

The little mother came through the ordeal surprisingly well, mostly because the calf was very, very small. He was also very weak and limp. His head lolled in the grass, his legs sprawled at odd angles, his eyes were only half open and each shallow breath threatened to be his last.

Like most farmers we are compelled to nurture even the faintest spark of life. We put the immature mother in the squeeze and milked her. She gave us a scant cupful and while Ralph held up the calf's head I dribbled the milk into his inert throat.

"Think he'll make it till morning?" I asked.

My husband shrugged. "Just as well if he doesn't. He's probably premature, too weak to suck and even if he does get on his feet she won't have enough milk to feed him."

On Tuesday the calf was just as floppy and uncoordinated. He lay as we had left him, head lolling, barely breathing, but still alive. We put his mother in the squeeze again and milked out another cupful. I put the milk in a bottle, and while Ralph held up the calf's head I pushed the nipple into its cold, unresponsive mouth. Very slowly and weakly it began to suck.

We now had a semi-live calf and no food for it. I went over to see my friend Mary, who milks cows, and borrowed frozen colostrum and a quart of whole milk. Every four hours I put a cup of warm milk–colostrum mix in a bottle and fed "my calf." I had to prop his head with one hand and push the nipple into his mouth with the other. With each feeding I imagined that he nursed more strongly, more nearly held up his own head. If I arranged his legs in standard calf position he looked almost normal. I didn't get much else done on Tuesday, what with warming milk, holding the bottle while he nursed, trotting back and forth to check on his breathing and rearranging his legs.

On Wednesday morning he really did hold up his own head. I was tremendously encouraged and went over to Mary's and got two quarts of milk. By Wednesday afternoon he was getting up on his back legs and falling forward onto his face. Every time I went to feed him, his poor little mouth was full of dirt. I didn't get much done on Wednesday either. I didn't have to check his breathing or rearrange his legs but I did have to haul him back on the grass when he flopped into the dirt and I had to clean the mud out of his mouth.

On Thursday I went into town for a bag of milk replacer suitable for newborns. By afternoon, if I stood him up he could stay there for a few minutes. You can see I didn't get much done on Thursday.

On Friday he took his first step. I was so thrilled that I kept running back and forth to see how he was managing. He kept blundering into fences and falling down, but he didn't give up.

On Saturday it began to rain. I tried to persuade the other members of this family to share with me the joy of watching that shiny little black body bloom but none of them wanted to deprive me of the solitary pleasure. I slogged out through the mud and fed him myself.

On Sunday nine-year-old Lee and six-year-old Kate were here and they just loved bottle-feeding a calf. I was happy to give them this opportunity.

On Monday the cats discovered me standing there in the rain and muck holding a bottle of milk. The cats wanted the milk and attempted to climb my bare legs, and the dogs, attracted by my screams, tried to annihilate the cats. The calf was now strong enough to nuzzle and slobber all over my clothes. It was awful.

On Tuesday evening my daughter offered to feed the calf. Gratefully I gave her the measurements. She put the milk replacer and warm water into a half-gallon jar, then instead of stirring the mix she just put the lid on tight and shook it. The jar exploded and a piece of glass sliced into her wrist and severed a tendon. She needed several stitches, a splint and a sling.

On Wednesday the doctor assured us that Kirsten's hand would be just fine. Meanwhile the calf continued to be wonderfully healthy and to grow like crazy. And by Thursday, I thought it was possible that I too would survive.

Driving Lessons

I DRIVE BECAUSE I have to. My husband certainly doesn't have time to do all the errands and it seems that every day holds at least one commitment that requires transportation by car.

My driving ability is questionable—even I know that I am not a "natural." My mind wanders and I have been known to amble along two miles beyond my destination. Twice I have overshot a Women's Institute meeting, only coming to my senses when I met another member on the road. Heaven knows what would have happened if I hadn't met anyone. I would probably have driven into town, bought groceries, paid the gas bill and dropped off last month's secretary's minutes at the newspaper.

I learned to drive under dreadful conditions. My dad was a wonderful horseman but a dubious mechanic so he wasn't willing to teach us. My older brothers were away from home and wouldn't trust us with their vehicles anyway, so when my brother Howie and I reached driving age, we "borrowed" Dad's Plymouth and taught ourselves. Once or twice my sister Marjie came along, but she was terrible and we both went home shaking and screaming.

"Bearing down from the left!" she'd shriek, and I'd stand on both brake and clutch while the car whipped wildly from one side to the other of the gravel road. When we had come to a smoking halt, stalled the Plymouth and removed our faces from the steering wheel and dashboard, sure enough there was a car on our left, about half a mile away and travelling a good 15 mph.

"Do you hear that?" she would ask in a voiced filled with doom.

"What? What?" I'd ask, preparing to stand on the brakes again.

"That pocketa, pocketa, clunk sound," she'd reply. "Our car sounded just like that before the transmission went out. Oh, Dad's gonna kill you. Does he know you have the car?"

I must have been desperate even to consider asking her to teach me. She's the one who drove a truck five miles in low gear at full throttle. When she finally stopped, the truck was so hot that the paint was all curled up on the gas gauge and speedometer. She denies it but I'm quite sure that she's the one who told me that a right turn is signalled by the passenger sticking his arm out of his window. That was pre-signal lights, of course, and she still doesn't trust them. Recently when the two of us were out and a man approaching the intersection from my left was signalling a right turn, I assumed that it was safe for me to turn right and I began to move forward. "Don't trust him!" Marjie yelled, reaching for her door handle. "Sometimes they hit those switches by accident."

Despite my instructors I finally dared to take the car downtown and attempt parallel parking. A friendly passerby began giving me directions—he stood at the front of the car where it was nosed out into the street and made elaborate turning motions with his hands. Sometimes he beckoned me forward, sometimes he pushed his palm against an imaginary object and I obediently reversed. This went on for several minutes while traffic backed up and I grew nauseated and sweaty-palmed. When I couldn't take it any more I rolled down the window.

"Never mind," I told him. "I'll go park it on a lot."

"Park it!" he said looking embarrassed. "I thought you were trying to get out."

My kids all took Alberta Motor Association driving lessons—I insisted on it.

THE MEADOWLARK

A FIRST IMPRESSION of Bill Crook, who is married to my husband's sister Edna, is all strength, mass and rugged charm. At family parties, among the soft-spoken, quiet Olsons, others may bring serenity and beauty, but Bill and I provide the noise, colour and dumb jokes. He has massive shoulders, a barrel chest and huge hands. He is also intelligent, sensitive, kind and gentle.

On their farm in the foothills at Pincher Creek, Bill and Edna raise sheep. One early spring morning Bill was out checking his lambs when he saw a pair of meadowlarks. Few birds have a more distinctive call and to hear a meadowlark sing is a delight, so Bill was pleased to see this pair. But they were behaving very strangely. The female would spread one wing, flutter wildly along the ground and then fall back, exhausted. The male would make a short flight away from her, call loudly and return to her side. He did this several times while Bill watched.

At Bill's approach, the birds became frantic. The male was obviously urging his mate to flight, and she just as plainly wished to fly, but could not. She was so worn out that she scarcely struggled as Bill caught her. He thought that her wing was broken, but as he stroked and gentled her, he found no external injury. Then, as he spread her useless wing, he realized that the problem was in her shoulder. Very gently, he manipulated the wing and was thrilled to hear a soft *snap* as the joint popped into place. He held her quietly for a few more minutes, then opened his hands, and the meadowlark lady flew away into the sky.

The male watched her go, but he didn't follow immediately. First he flew twice around Bill's head, then he settled himself on a nearby post, swelled his chest and sang and sang an ecstasy of meadowlark songs. Three times he went through his repertoire, and Bill was overwhelmed by this rare and beautiful performance.

Because of the distinct syllables in a meadowlark song, people have attempted to translate it into English. Phyllis Hunt's meadowlarks say, "Oh you dirty, dirty boy." To Rosetta MacFarquhar they say, "Plant your sweet potatoes," followed by "Pull 'em up by the roots." Pearl Stone hears, "Is that my sister? That's my sister."

And somewhere near Pincher Creek, a meadowlark says, "Thank you, big, good, gentle Bill."

HUB-DEEP IN *M*UD

I WAS FOLDING laundry at the kitchen counter and Ralph had gone to feed cows, so I was surprised to hear his footsteps on the deck and the kitchen door opening. "I need you to come and help me," he said. I finished rolling a big blue bath towel, checked that the coffee pot and stove were turned off and reached for my gloves and coat. We were outside before I asked him where we were going.

"I'm stuck," he said grimly.

I stopped walking. "Stuck!" I said incredulously. "It's dry as a bone out here, wouldn't getting stuck take an act of extreme stupidity?"

"Yes it would," he agreed, "and that's why I don't want to hear another word about it."

It was cozy, both of us and the huge nylon tow rope packed into the tractor cab and rolling across the greening pasture. It was certainly more pleasant than most of the trips we have taken toward a "stuck" site. I wasn't supposed to talk but I could think, and I began remembering other times that the two of us had manoeuvred our way out of stuck situations.

Our first combine was a faded red Cockshutt and it was all we could afford at the time. It was self-propelled, looked about fifteen feet tall and had no cab. The tires weren't the best and it was a wet fall. How I hated that tall, tippy-looking combine, and when one side of it sank lower than the other, my beloved young husband looked like the captain of a storm-tossed, sinking schooner who was prepared to go down with the ship. I, on my cabless tractor and connected to the hulk by a long chain, inched along and prayed that the miserable thing would not upset. Ralph, in his crow's nest perch, signalled, "Go, go, hurry up, move." But I could not "hurry up." What if it tipped over? How could I extricate him from under it? Would I try to dig him out by myself or go for help while he lay there trapped? Maybe I would watch him going down, have a heart attack and leave the kids orphans.

Hundreds of loads of gravel have gone on our lane since we first came here. I'm sure we used to have more snow too, because in the early years, just getting in from the road was a continuing challenge from November to June. John was a baby and Mark not yet two when we came back from visiting my folks to find the lane totally clogged with snow. While the little boys and I waited, Ralph went for the tractor and I tried to entertain a restless and cranky Mark. "Here we are in a big train," I told him. "Pretty soon the train will start and we will go to Calgary. Can you hear the engine? Chugga, chugga, there goes the whistle, whoooo, whoooo ... "

"This not a train," Mark interrupted. "It's a stupid car and Ralph gone for a tractor to pull she out."

A tractor mired hub-deep in a feedlot is about as unpleasant as it gets, especially if it's in a tight corner where you can't get it with one pull and have to reattach the filthy chain while standing in pools of slop. For a real lesson in fortitude and endurance, try cleaning up a drill after it has been through a session in a soft spot. I have never done this myself, or even helped with it. My husband prefers to do this sort of thing without an audience.

There is a period in early spring when the top foot or so has thawed and is soft and wet, and the earth below that is still frozen and hard and slippery. Oh then be wary all farmers with tractors, and wives should hide under the bed. I can think of at least three occasions on which I was sure that the situation was totally hopeless. Me in the tractor ahead and feeling the back tires slipping from side to side and sinking ever deeper, and then maybe gaining an inch and slipping again, and Ralph signalling go, go, and the whole world is noise and fumes and heart in the throat.

But this latest operation was a nice easy pull, straightforward, and I could stay on dry grass. Ralph had got stuck when he was looking for a clean place to feed the cows and a low spot that he had cut across before was softer than it looked. I didn't say a word. Getting stuck is part of farming, and stupidity has very little to do with it.

MY CAREER AS AN *E*GG GRADER

FOR ONE VERY interesting week, an Alberta radio station ran a contest that people entered by phoning in to tell about the worst job they ever had. One lady said she had been a barmaid in a tough little pub in Nova Scotia where her least favourite chore was "chasing the keg." This involved washing out barrels in a slimy basement. She stayed with the job for several years so there must have been some rewards. Another woman described her first and worst job—at age fourteen she worked for three weeks putting foam pads in padded bras. She was bored out of her mind. Another caller had been a busgirl in a busy restaurant during Stampede week and had broken crockery and spilled things on people for ten panic-filled days.

Awful jobs all of them, and nothing I'd care to do, but I'll bet my worst job was even worse.

I was sixteen, working in the Ponoka Co-op dry goods department and looking for something more challenging. My brother Ronny's friend Stan, the manager of the local creamery, told Ronny that the Alpha Dairies plant in Red Deer had job openings and paid well.

My cousin Dott drove me to Red Deer for the interview. She was seventeen and still learning to drive, so it took forever. When we got to the outskirts of Red Deer and saw the sign saying "25 mph" she had to speed up.

The Alpha plant manager was very nice, kind of fatherly and benign. He inquired after Stan and my brother, and now that we had established this friendly relationship he offered me some advice. The position in the office was okay but it was, after all, just an ordinary office job. If I really wanted a "career" I should snap up a golden opportunity that by an incredible stroke of luck had arisen that very week. There was a vacancy in their apprentice egg-grading program, and if I were to meet this challenge the world would open before me.

"From Boston to Zanzibar," he said, "there are egg-grading stations offering big wages and Easter bonuses to graduates of this program." He made a career in egg grading sound better than one in diplomatic service. Why, I wondered with growing excitement, would anyone go into law or medicine when egg grading was so obviously the wave of the future?

On the first day of my new career, I reported for duty wearing a grey pleated skirt and white nylon blouse, and nylons with high-heeled white sandals. Someone directed me to a flight of dark, cold concrete steps and at the foot of them I paused to let my eyes adjust to the gloom.

The ceiling was low and the lighting poor. There were no windows. Grey concrete walls dripped moisture into stagnant pools. Egg crates, forty-eight dozen to a crate, were stacked six feet high around the walls. These were arranged according to eggs that were ungraded, those that were graded and ready to be boxed and those that were graded, boxed and waiting to be picked up by delivery men. The actual egg-grading machine with all its belts, lights and pulleys clanked and rumbled centre stage and attached to it was a black, curtained enclosure that was a cross between a shower stall and an 1890s photographer's hood. This was the egg-graders' cubicle and from it emerged a gnarled, dark, troll-like creature named Jock. Besides me, only one of my three fellow employees was actually in the apprentice program. I guessed that the others had been unable to pass some test involving hard things like remembering your phone number. They all wore sweatshirts and jeans and looked as if they had not seen sunlight in years. They were not friendly. The word "troglodyte" comes to mind.

On the first day I ruined my nylons, broke all my fingernails and learned how to carry sixty-pound boxes through pools of water. On about my fourth day the troll approached, looked up from under his beetling brows and said, "arghl neugal grundegey uch ken licht." One of the assistant trolls translated this as an invitation to his cell.

Inside the dark cubicle he produced more guttural sounds, snatched three eggs in each of his grimy paws and began rotating them against a tiny bright spot of light.

For the next several days I shifted between hauling boxes, spinning eggs and trying to count by twelves. I hated all of these tasks equally.

On the eleventh day I showed up very late for work and the troglodytes gleefully rubbed their chapped little paws together and told me that the manager wanted to see me in the office.

Manager: "Do you get paid from 8:00 or 9:00 AM?"

Me: "From the salary I thought it was about noon."

Manager: "Are you not happy here?"

Me: "A brain-damaged chimpanzee would love it here."

Manager: "And you don't?"

That was the end of my career as an egg grader, and from egg-grading stations around the world, a little sigh of sorrow issued forth.

ßOVINE SNOWBOARDING

TWO YEARS AGO Ralph and I decided to quit finishing our own calves—we shipped them soon after weaning and did not keep back any heifers. Our herd was big enough for our pasture, and we were getting to the age when we should be taking things a little easier. Last fall, when the dust had settled after the weaning, sorting and shipping festivities, a nice little bunch of calves remained in the corral.

"Are you planning to finish these yourself?" I asked.

"No, not really," Ralph replied.

"Are we keeping them all as heifers, then?"

"Uh, no."

"Well, what then?" I persisted. "I thought we were trimming our herd, I thought we were going to aim for a couple more hassle-free, heiferless seasons and then quit. There is no way we can eat this many and they don't make good pets."

Ralph rested his hand on a gatepost and looked out over the pretty little group of red and black calves. "A couple of them were late arrivals and they are still pretty small," he said. "We have to ship a few old cows and that means there will be extra pasture, so it seems a shame not to have some heifers to eat the grass. I saved the one with the white tail because you especially like her mother."

Apparently we were still in the calving business. When we become residents of the old folks' home, I wonder if they will let us keep a couple of cows on the sundeck?

The calving season is synonymous with spring. It's new life, innocence and beauty, renewal, rebirth and faith. It's proof that once again nature has blessed the earth with the miracle of life. It's love in the form of a mother defending her baby, and the purest innocence in all those huge, long-lashed eyes. It is also late-night and early-morning walks, hope, fear, gratitude, mud, blood and mess.

We had no heifers the next year, so we had a fairly uncomplicated season. A backward presentation needed a bit of help and resulted in a fine live calf and a nice black cow delivered twin red babies and liked them both. Things were going almost too well. Then a big snow came along to complicate everybody's mobility, and somehow a nice little bull calf got his leg broken. Ralph took him to the vet's and there they decided that even though the break was above the knee and therefore less easily mended, they would cast it and hope for the best. The calf was going to need painkiller shots for a few days and penicillin shots for a few days after that, but first Ralph returned him to the pasture so that we could use him to lure his mother (and food source) up to the corrals.

We attached our heavy plastic calf sled to the back of the tractor. Ralph and the calf lay on the sled with their various limbs arranged as painlessly as possible. The cow bellowed in our wake and Ralph signalled me to go. There were several cows and calves ahead of me on the trail and deep, deep snow on either side. Running over three healthy calves to save one damaged one didn't seem like good economics, so I crept along waiting for the trail to clear. When I glanced back at my beloved husband he was making "hurry up" signals, so as soon as the way was clear, I shifted gears and hurried up. The calf sloop did not conform to the path made by the tractor tires—it tended to slew from side to side. Some quite large puddles had formed. I tried to avoid the largest ones but it was pointless, so I just drove, checking occasionally to make sure that no one had fallen off or been bashed by the cow. Ralph was making more hand signals, but I think he does Norwegian hand signals and I only understand about three out of ten. The cow was coming along fine so I sped up a little more. Up the hills we churned snow and through the draws we hydroplaned. The sloop careened madly from side to side but the passengers stayed aboard. I whipped through the pasture gate and slowed to a stop. The cow was still with us and I was well pleased with our progress. Ralph was making hand signals again. It was a set I had never seen before.

It turns out that the signal for "slow down" becomes somewhat distorted when you are lying down with a calf in one hand, a pitchfork in the other, a cow bawling in your ear and a face full of ice water. It turns out that Ralph was not cleverly using his right leg as a stabilizer and rudder but was unable to regain purchase on the sled because of the speed at which we were travelling. It turns out that tractor competitions do not have a Cow–Calf Snowboarding Event, but if they did, we would be among the contenders.

Ralph and the calf were both soaking wet and very cold, but their outlooks improved as they dried off, neither of them developed pneumonia, and the calf's leg healed beautifully.

A $\mathcal{S}$LITHERY SOUND

WHEN I WAS growing up, the 24th of May was a time to celebrate, a sort of "welcome summer" time. It was the first dance at Sylvan Lake, a live band and a chance to meet friends you hadn't seen since the last 24th of May. It was a tradition, for heaven's sake.

Meanwhile my husband was growing up in a family that viewed May 24 as the time to plant potatoes. If spring was early the potatoes could go in sooner, but May 24 was the traditional time for planting them and if the day was nice and the garden soil warm, everything but the corn and beans went in as well.

Guess whose tradition endured? Ralph's mom and dad loved this place and loved to garden. They seem awfully close at this time of year.

We have occasionally experimented with planting times. Twice, in the hope of really early vegetables, I seeded carrots, lettuce and spinach in the fall. There was no advantage. In the spring, we put the main garden in at the regular time. None of the seeds germinated until the soil was warmed and by that time both spring and fall sown plants were equally advanced, but the weeds were bigger in the fall planting because the soil there had not been disturbed. One very early spring we planted most of the garden in the middle of April. I will never do that again. The weed seeds had not yet germinated and so the rototiller did not kill them. Eight billion chickweeds came up with the carrots and had to be laboriously hand-pulled. Groundsel hid among the lettuce and flung seeds into the pea rows, vetch grew along with the corn and bound leaves to stalks while thistles, lush as young willows, came up everywhere. So we went back to "on or before May 24." It's a good rule for this part of the country.

One year I decided to plant alyssum from seed. This is not my usual method—normally I buy ten or twelve flats of alyssum—but my sister-in-law grows it satisfactorily from seed and that year I wanted to see if it would work in my garden. I tucked the three packages of seed into the breast pocket of my shirt, put on my shoes and gloves and then remembered that I had some nasturtium seeds soaking and that they should be planted first. I left the dish of wet nasturtium seeds on the steps while I prepared a place for them. Two of the tubs that I plant nasturtiums in were a bit low on soil, and it was while I was scooping earth from the garden into the wheelbarrow that I first heard the sneaky, mysterious sound. It was a soft sound but sort of menacing. A whispery, slithery sound and not one that I could remember having heard before. I stopped shovelling and listened very carefully. Birds sang, leaves rustled in the breeze, a small plane buzzed somewhere to the east. The slithery sound had stopped.

Off and on during the afternoon the sound came back. I would be bent double placing seeds in a row and the whispery sound would seem close enough to touch, but the moment I stopped what I was doing and listened quietly, it ceased. I heard it when I was near the spruce trees watering in the newly planted nasturtiums. I heard it when I bent to make the rows for the alyssum. It began to sound like a series of quick steps in dry leaves. Like a snake in thick undergrowth. Like a cougar snuffling human scent. Like a giant bat caught in a pail. I like being alone and it takes a lot to frighten me, but why did it stop whenever I stood still and listened? Whatever it was, it was aware of me and was watching. I was beginning to get nervous. I was tempted to find something to do in the house until my husband came home, but I was so close to finishing and darn it, this was the 22nd of May and the last of the seeds had to be in the ground before the 24th. I reached into my pocket for the packets of seed. The slithery sound was very close now—in fact it was in my hand. The mystery was solved. A large package of alyssum seeds carried in your shirt pocket makes a slithery sound when you bend over and straighten up but goes perfectly silent when you stop moving. Next year I will buy my alyssum as bedding plants.

SOMETHING HAS TO BE
DONE WITH THE ßATHROOM

WHEN RALPH AND I added the guest room and bath, our existing bathroom lost its window. Actually it lost the glass from its window—the frame and sill were still there. As a temporary measure I pinned a *National Geographic* close-up of a shark's face into the opening and told the kids to pretend they were on an ocean voyage and their cabins were below decks.

The shark hung there "temporarily" for about four years. By last fall he was decidedly faded and water-stained. Besides that, the ceramic-coated hardboard that surrounded the tub was starting to decay and the grooves in the panelled areas were beginning to look dark and fuzzy. Something would have to be done with the bathroom.

Shortly after we realized this, the hot water tap in the main bathroom sink began to leak so alarmingly that Ralph had to plug off the line. Because we could use only cold water, the drain soon congealed and the sink became utterly useless. By this time we knew that replacement taps for this model were no longer available, so there was no point in opening the drain.

This bathroom backs onto the guest bath, which has a shower and sink but, because of a concrete foundation and old sewer lines, no toilet. After about ten days of using one bathroom for the toilet and the other for the sink, I watched Ralph prepare for morning chores and made a suggestion.

"When you come in for lunch, honey," I said, "bring along the axe."

"Any special reason?" he asked.

"I thought I'd chop through the wall and make one full bath from these two miserable halves," I told him.

"That's okay with me," he said. "Just don't trip and break a leg when you walk through the tub on your way to the sink.

"Actually," he continued, "I have a plan for your darn bathroom. I am going to bring in the jigsaw and cut a half moon over the door.

Then you can quit thinking of it as a poor bathroom and start being grateful that your outdoor biffy is inside where it's warm."

We are both reasonable people (one slightly more than the other), so confrontation led to peaceful negotiation.

"I will be as economical as possible," I told him. "Not everything has to be changed."

"Does this mean that you will settle for a new sink?" he asked.

"Of course not," I countered. "You know that the walls around the tub are falling apart. I want Ceramalite there again. It stands up pretty well—the old stuff lasted for about fifteen years."

"Almost unbelievable," Ralph answered. "If it had been bolted to the hull of the *Queen Mary* it wouldn't have had to shed more water than it has in our bathroom. You can have new wallboard if I can put in a fan to cut down the moisture."

"I'll go for the fan," I offered, "if you incorporate it in a new light and get a more expensive one. The first one you put in the guest bath was so loud that when my sister accidentally hit the switch she thought she was in a helicopter and started looking around for the airsick bag."

"Any further demands?" he asked crisply. "Or can we consider this a contract?"

"There are a few more things," I smiled, "but before I present them I want to come to an agreement on bargaining tactics. If I promise not to cry and quit speaking to you, will you promise not to swear and kick doors?"

"This sounds like a big one," he said. "I had better sit down."

"It starts with the bathtub," I began. "It is thirty-five years old and won't come clean any more. I want a new bathtub, and it's foolish to pull the tub without putting down new linoleum. If everything else is new then I want new cupboards, a bigger medicine chest and a new mirror. The old one is a mess."

"How about the towel pole?" he asked weakly.

"Sorry," I told him. "I have blue enamel in mind."

"Holder for the toilet paper?"

"It ought to match the towel bar," I said gently.

He reached for pen and paper and began to make a list. "Is it too late," he asked, "to go back to the half-moon-in-the-door plan?"

*V*ANILLA THROUGH THE AGES

— 1966 —

"WHAT'S 'AT, MOMMY?"

"That's vanilla, sweetheart. Here, smell it, doesn't it smell good? Makes the icing taste yummy. Can you say *vanilla?* Vah-nill-ah."

— 1969 —

"What's vanilla made from, Mommy?"

"Well, this is artificial vanilla, which means it's made from chemicals, I suppose. Real vanilla is made from vanilla beans."

"Beans like we grow in the garden?"

"No, long, tough, black beans that smell delicious. Someday when we are in a fancy grocery store I'll show you some vanilla beans. They come in long, thin glass tubes."

"Do you cook the vanilla beans?"

"I think you put the bean in with some sugar and then when you use the sugar it's already flavoured."

"You sure are a smart Mommy."

— 1973 —

"Mom, did you know that this vanilla is made from the pods of tropical climbing orchids?"

"Really."

"Did you know that the Aztecs used it to make a drink?"

"Really."

"In fact, Cortes drank vanilla-flavoured chocolate at Montezuma's court!"

"For crying out loud, how do you know so much about vanilla?"

"Oh, Mrs. Erickson told us in school. Boy, she sure is a smart teacher."

— 1976 —

"Grandma says she only uses pure vanilla. Why do you use artificial?"

"Artificial is half the price, that's why, and it tastes the same as far as I can tell."

"Have you got any idea what's in artificial vanilla? Do you know that practically everything you buy contains chemicals? Do you realize that a lot of the additives and preservatives in processed foods are suspected carcinogens? Look at this: propylene glycol, do you know what propylene glycol is? For all you know it's rat poison."

"So don't eat the whipped cream, then. I don't suppose the pure food and drug people would allow rat poison in vanilla—we poor stupid housewives have to trust a higher authority."

— 1982 —

"Do you know what this is, Mom?"

"It better be vanilla, otherwise I've been putting cough syrup in the cookies."

"Oh, it's vanilla all right, but do you know what it is?"

"You'd better just tell me, honey, it's obvious that you know something I don't."

"Okay, it's 3-methoxy, 4-hydroxy benzaldehyde."

"What?"

"That's the IUPAC standardized name for vanillin."

"IUPAC?"

"International Union of Pure and Applied Chemists."

"Thanks, dear, I really needed that."

"It's okay, Mom, I knew you'd appreciate it. Want me to draw the structural formula?"

"Oh, please do. Draw it in my cookbook and I'll refer to it every time I bake."

I'm proud of the kids' intelligence, and I appreciate modern education. But my, I miss those brief days when I was a smart Mommy.

OVER THE TOP IN THE *G*ARDEN

ONCE THERE WAS a fairly normal, reasonably happy lady who liked to keep a neat garden. She liked nice clean edges on her flower beds, she hated grass growing anywhere other than the lawn, she could not tolerate one plant creeping into another and she especially disliked spent blooms on her flowering plants. She spent hours following grass roots into primulas and columbines and then removing them with the dedication of a brain surgeon. She was heartless about grubbing sweet-faced pansies out from under her rose bushes, and petunia blossoms had scarcely begun to wilt when she snapped them off and dropped them into her compost bin.

"Anything that's growing where it doesn't belong is a weed," she told herself grimly as she yanked up another pansy or hoed down a patch of poppies. Her forget-me-nots and lily of the valley were relegated to a bit of grass under a tree because they spread so badly that she would not have them in a flower bed, and after her bad experience with the invasive blue flax she wouldn't have it anywhere. She could recognize a two-inch flax plant from a distance of forty paces. All flax plants were immediately destroyed.

She knew the names of all her flowers and she knew the names of all her weeds. Stinkweed, groundsel, henbit, clover, dandelion, chickweed, pigweed, thistle—she chanted their names like a mantra. Her spade and trowel were never far from her hand, her faithful dandelion digger never really cooled off, she was relentless, ruthless and ultimately exhausted, but still she pursued every grass root, every plant of whatever ilk, if it grew where it didn't belong.

Dogs and cats were allowed to walk sedately among her flower beds but never in them, and any dog that even contemplated burying something was putting his life at risk. When deer ate her rosebuds and a moose chewed on a willow tree, she de-posted her land, and sometimes on really dark nights she would black out the NO on her neighbour's NO HUNTING signs.

Not all guests were welcome in the garden, and small children were regarded with thinly veiled distrust. A sedate game of bean bag toss was occasionally allowed on the lawn, but no one played catch in the garden and no one threw frisbees either. Her family had mixed emotions about her gardening. Yes, it looked nice, but occasionally there were murmured words, like "compulsive," "crabby," "fanatic" and "obsessive." Still, they loved her, and because she had other less unfortunate qualities, they tolerated her fixation and mostly overlooked it, as long as the problem stayed at home.

And then she began going public. "Do you mind?" she said as she pulled stinkweeds from the ornamental stone display at the garden centre. "Are you going to let that groundsel go to seed?" she asked the caretaker at city hall. "These bloom longer and better if you remove the spent blossoms," she told a shop owner at the mall. She was picking deadheads off his petunias at the time. In friends' gardens she surreptitiously picked seed heads from pansies and snapped overblown blooms from geraniums. One day, while she was using her nail file to furiously dig grass from a bed of junipers in front of the Dairy Queen, three men in white coats arrived and took her away. As she was being led into the hospital psychiatric wing she broke loose and ripped four male blossoms from a begonia. "Now the female flowers will grow larger," she assured the attendants.

She has a lovely room. It's filled with flowers. All plastic, of course. There are no weeds, no wilting blooms, no slugs, no dandelions or groundsel, no grass insinuating its sneaky roots into the primula. Once in a while she waters them.

THE *W*ARDROBE COORDINATOR

AT ALBERTA WOMEN'S INSTITUTE workshops we study some unpleasant but compelling social issues. The fight against pornography is one of our priorities, as is assistance for victims of family violence, education against child sexual abuse, conservation, leadership—the list is a long one. All of these are areas where WI has made a difference, lobbying, educating and contributing time and money.

A few years ago we decided to give ourselves a break from all these worldly cares and booked one fun evening. The fun speaker was young, female, very attractive, very thin and beautifully clothed and groomed. Her subject was fashion, and some of the less fashionable among us viewed her with vague alarm. What would a part-time model, fashion consultant, wardrobe coordinator and professional shopper have in common with overweight, budget-conscious women who sew their own clothes?

"Out of Africa is the look for this season," she told us. "Khaki is the predominant colour in both the green and brown tones and accessories should be in red, peach and black."

I'm in luck, I thought. I have two items of khaki clothing—the bra and slip that I accidentally washed with a green blouse. Not much to build a wardrobe around, but it's a start. As for accessories, I have three long red scarves left from the kids' County Band days and a peach-and-brown-striped toque that I keep in the car for emergencies, and I carry my big, black purse year-round.

"For summer," she continued, "look for brown with white, white with cream, white with navy, white with pastels—in fact, white with everything. This is the time to buy a white skirt and white pants," she continued, "and make sure they are lined."

My friend Kathy leaned toward me and whispered, "Finally I can use that imitation blue and white eyelet that I bought in 1980. I thought I'd have to make it into bathroom curtains."

"She said white with blue," I told Kathy, "not blue and white print. You had better make up the curtains, or maybe you could line your white pants with it."

"I don't think so," she said sadly. "The blue spots would show through and I'd look 'out of Africa' all right, sort of like a snow leopard."

The speaker had finished with colour trends and was explaining her work as wardrobe coordinator and professional shopper.

"My fee is thirty dollars an hour," she told us, "and here is how I earn it. First I go into the client's home and she and I sort through her closet. Anything that has not been worn for three years, goes. If it has great sentimental value she can store it, otherwise it's given away."

"I can imagine what she'd say if she looked in my closet," I told Kathy. "She'd either faint or collapse laughing."

"Next," our speaker continued, "I list what's left by type and colour, and I evaluate the client's lifestyle and fashion type. Then I take some of the major items with me so that I can match colours and I call on several stores and have them put away things I choose in my client's size. Finally, the client and I call at the stores and she tries on the clothes that I have chosen."

"It sounds lovely," Kathy sighed, "and it sure beats my method, which involves running into the store at closing time, snatching up a few sale items and hoping that they will fit either me or my daughter."

"Nothing so haphazard for me," I replied loftily. "I have clothes buying down to a science. First I buy fabric that I don't really like but feel I can afford, then I store it for up to two years or until the eve of some event that absolutely demands a new dress. I then make the dress and hate it, but wear it anyway out of desperation. Three years later the thing is faded and threadbare and has become my favourite garment."

"You obviously need a shopper," Kathy observed. "When may I come to inspect your closet?"

"Go home and line your white pants," I told her.

BEAU THE CATTLE DOG

BEAU WAS AN AWKWARD and adorable puppy that grew into a sleek, agile, bright and very handsome dog. So he brought rocks, sticks, grease rags and horrible long-dead things to the front lawn—he also guarded, retrieved and caught. I admit he ruined a patch of clarkia playing "bouncing for bees," but he also learned very quickly not to run through flower beds. He did make a terrible mess when he dug up the firepit, but how many dogs help dig potatoes and pick their own peas?

The time came when Beau was old enough to begin some serious training. I hauled him into an empty granary and, using a rope for judicious mild smacks, I taught him Sit, Stay and Here in about five minutes. We moved outside and continued. He was a joy to teach. I discarded my switch and worked him using only love and praise. "He is brilliant," I told my husband. "He responds instantly when I say *Here*."

On a Wednesday evening early in his training we let some cattle into a freshly combined field near the house and Beau and I walked out to see them. There were about a hundred head of various ages, and while I admired them Beau slipped under the fence and trotted toward the herd. He wasn't accustomed to seeing cattle here and was understandably curious. A couple of chunky black heifers tossed their heads and pretended to charge him. Beau backed away; they snorted and followed.

I was a little disappointed in him. A cattle dog should not be afraid of cattle. The heifers lowered their heads and threatened him. Beau slipped under the fence and sat by my feet.

I sized up the situation—a nice clear field with lots of room to run, and since Beau is so beautifully trained to come back when called . . .

The heifers danced a little and tossed their pretty heads. "Sic 'em, Beau," I said quietly. Beau put his head to one side and looked up at me. I repeated the order and gestured at the cattle. Like a bullet he launched himself into the startled heifers. They backed off, Beau gained confidence and barked authoritatively, the heifers turned and ran.

I was delighted. "Here, Beau," I called confidently, but Beau, drunk with power and missionary zeal, ignored me.

With the heifers in flight, he swept up the next group and started them running. "Beau!" I screamed. "Here! *Here!*" But he was beyond my control and having a wonderful time, almost silent and seeming to be everywhere at once—sweeping, gathering, dropping back for stragglers. They were all running and bawling now, and my hysterical screams had absolutely no effect on cows or dog.

By this time the lead animals were funnelling through a gate and into an adjoining field. Several calves seemed to be heading for certain disaster and I expected to hear rending wire when they hit the fence. But Beau faded left and redirected them, and they slipped through the gate unharmed. Now a band of trees impeded my view but I could glimpse occasional running bodies. Though it seemed hopeless and stupid, I was still screaming, "Here, Beau! Here, here!"

In a matter of seconds the runners broke free from the trees and I could see Beau gathering them and changing direction. Then, in a long, undulating stream, they flowed into their old familiar pasture.

A small black form broke from the herd and came toward me. It was Beau. Now that he had put the cows back where they belonged, he was coming home. I was so grateful that nothing had been killed and no fences torn out, and I was so exhausted from screaming, I could scarcely punish him.

"Beau and I did a little work with the cows today," I told my husband. "I think you'd have been surprised at his performance."

SCANDAL AND ROMANCE

IN 1922 MARTHA MATTERN was twenty years old. She was very beautiful, the daughter of a respectable and conservative family, a clerk at Edward's Dry Goods Store in Ponoka, and she was engaged to an upstanding young man whose intentions were honourable and prospects assured.

One evening the young man walked Martha home to the door of her Aunt Tilly's house, bestowed upon her a chaste kiss, swallowed twice as if he were trying to say something or maybe his celluloid collar was too tight, turned on his well-polished heel and walked away into the dark summer night. They never met again.

Part of the reason that I have always loved this story is because the man had such a fine romantic name—Sterling Danford, right out of a Victorian novel. It seems Sterling had taken one of his company cheques for $100 and artfully converted it to $1,000. This gave him a nice little profit of $900, but it cost him his reputation, his job, his family and his girl. He ran away to Oklahoma, wrote Martha and begged her to meet him there, but she ignored his letters, took off his engagement ring and, with head held high, endured the ensuing scandal.

Aunt Tilly got the idea that the police would confiscate the diamond ring so she hid it in the flour bin. Fortunately the ring had been paid for pre-theft so no one ever asked for it and Aunt Tilly mercifully did not bake it into a biscuit.

In 1922 Glen Johnston was twenty-one. He had been raised within a dozen miles of Martha but they had attended different schools and as soon as he had finished school he had gone to his sister's at Chinook to be a farmhand and cowboy. About the time that Aunt Tilly deemed it safe to remove the ring from the flour bin, Glen came back to Ponoka to visit his father and his brother Fay. The two boys strolled downtown and chanced to pass Edward's Store just as Martha placed something in the window display.

There on the sidewalk Glen halted in mid-stride and did a dramatic double take. "Fay," he said, "I have just seen the woman I am going to marry."

"Don't get your hopes up," Fay said. "That's Sterling Danford's widow and I don't think she is going out with other men yet."

They did marry and they had joy and sorrow, good times and bad. They had eight children; seven of us survive. They sold Sterling's ring to buy groceries during the Depression but except for that one involuntary contribution he was not part of our lives.

Once when my sister Marjie was cutting Dad's hair and finding the job very difficult because Dad insisted, as usual, "Shorter, shorter, trim some off while you're at it," Mom, equally insistent, said, "Leave a little down on his neck and don't cut the sideburns so short."

Suddenly Mom had an evil inspiration. She had been going through some things in the attic and if he wanted short hair, she'd show him short hair. "Here," she said, thrusting a photo under his nose. "Why don't you have her cut it like this?" And there, frozen in time, was Sterling Danford.

"Oh, I'm sorry," Mom said. "I shouldn't have done that, it was a nasty trick."

Dad shrugged his shoulders. "It's all right," he said. "After all, I'm the one who got the girl."

I have always been grateful to good old Sterling. If he hadn't raised that cheque and run off to Tulsa, Mom would never have married Dad, all our lives would have been entirely different and a lot of love would have been lost to the world.

NO BUSINESS LIKE *H*AY BUSINESS

WE LIVE IN THE MIDDLE of some of the best "hay country" in Canada, but this is also "cattle country."

For many years Ralph and I fed most of our hay to our own cattle and sold very little. Well, we had bumper crops in 1993 and '94, followed by mild winters (cows eat less when it's warm). We sold our feeders earlier than usual, and grain prices were awful so we expanded our hayland. The following spring we had a lot of hay, at our farm and at my sister-in-law Marie's place—more than we could possibly use.

"I think I'll put out some feelers and sell some of this hay," Ralph said. It seemed logical to me, but that was about the last logical thing in the whole operation.

There are several kinds of hay, at various locations. At Marie's it is stacked along the lane and south of the house. At our place the hay bales are lined up along the lane on the north side (through the north gate) and on the west side of the trees. We have more hay in several strategically placed fenced yards, but that is not for sale. There is '93 and '94 hay. There is coarse and fine hay, timothy, alfalfa, brome and mixed. There are self-loading trucks and trucks that require loading. Of the ones that require loading, one or two are so huge that our tractor's grasp exceeds its reach and Ralph can't set the top layer of the load. Some of the trucks are so long that they can't manage Marie's gate and have to be rerouted through a field. Some of the hay has gone through a dealer and some of it has been sold privately. Some of the trucking for private sales was arranged through the dealer. There are a lot of truckers, all of whom have mobile phones and need directions to and from places like Pollardville and Couleeview.

Some of the people involved give us their last names, some the first. One person has a name like Leslie Lloyd. I don't know which is last and which is first. At least three people are named Stuart or maybe Stewart. I don't know if I have Stuart the trucker or Stewart the buyer, or perhaps some luckless Stuart trying to sell carpet cleaning.

"This is my hay file," Ralph said, "and these top pages have the information you will need if anyone phones." I looked at his hay file with some suspicion. Farm husbands have a way of assuming that whatever they know, their wives know by osmosis or telepathy or maybe ESP. In agricultural communities all over the world, wives stand at parts counters while partsmen say things like, "Did he say if the frammelsnatch wound from the right or left, and is that with or without the optional gingelfridget?" I knew this was going to be one of those times.

"Just a minute," I told him. "This is a list of numbers and names. Who is trucking what, when and from where?"

"You never know who," he apologized, "because some truckers work only weekends, the Wilbur–Ellis people employ any number of truckers and some of the private sales may haul their own. As to what and from where, well, that depends on who is coming, doesn't it? And when depends on the trucker's schedule and the weather."

I sighed and prepared for trouble. As soon as he left the house, the phone began to ring. I put a new page on his hay file and took notes.

"Eric can help you load the High Boy," I told him, "and I think that's over at Marie's."

"When?" he asked.

I checked my notes. "I don't know. Today, I think. Clint says it depends on how long someone named Jimmy takes to get back from Ohaton. Someone named Eddie will be here at 2:00 for alfalfa."

"Here?" Ralph said. "The alfalfa is at Marie's."

"Sorry," I told him, "but I have some trucker's mobile number. Maybe it's his and maybe you can stop him. Phyllis called and gave me this name of someone who wants hay."

"What kind of hay?" he asked. "And where does this person live?"

"I don't know, I can only get his answering machine. Bill phoned to see if you can fill an order for one of his customers but I didn't know what we had left, so you will have to call him back. Someone named Stuart called and will come tomorrow morning if he doesn't hear otherwise."

"Stuart who?"

"I have no idea."

Ralph groaned softly, took my notes and perused them in some bewilderment. "Who are Bill C. Froyurt and Harry P?" he asked.

I looked over his shoulder. "That's black cherry frozen yogurt and Hawaiian pizza. It's my Schwan's order."

"Next year," he said grimly, "I will plow it all up, sow it to barley and market it through the Wheat Pool."

TINKERBELL *G*RANDMA

FOR ROLL CALL at our Women's Institute meetings, each member is required to answer a predetermined question when her name is called. This may seem like a frivolous pursuit, especially when the question is funny, but in actual practice it is an important part of the meeting. It forces every member to take part, even in a small way, and gives shy or new members an opportunity to contribute and gain confidence. We learn a lot from roll call. Subjects range from the ridiculous: "If you had a tattoo, where would you have it and what would it be?" to the sublime: "Nominate someone for the next book of remarkable Alberta women." A good roll call should involve some thought, maybe some research and often a vivid memory. Here is one of mine.

It was mid-May and my sisters Donna and Marj and I had stopped for lunch in a nice café that was filled with flowers and greenery. We had just been shown to our table when another group was ushered to the larger table beside us. The party was made up of two women in their early forties, five children ranging from about eight to fourteen and a more mature lady, probably in her mid-sixties. It was the older lady who seized our attention. She was an outdoor-type grandma, a bit on the bony side with deeply tanned and weathered skin, lots of wrinkles, and short, wiry, salt-and-pepper hair. The type of grandma who rides horses, plays golf, digs her own flower beds and wears blue jeans and boots. But this tough and wiry grandma was apparently in the throes of a serious mental breakdown.

She was wearing a dress made of a fluffy, filmy, pink fabric. The full, short skirt came just above her brown and bumpy knees, and the sleeves were very puffy and stuck up above her shoulders like little wing nubbins about to sprout. It was too big in the waist, too wide in the shoulders and too low in the back. This made the neckline too generous, and the dress kept slipping off first one shoulder and then the other. The neckline was trimmed in sequins, and she wore a wide gold belt and a matching pink sequin-trimmed bow in her hair. She had everything but the wand and fairy dust. She looked like the Tooth Fairy with a really bad hangover, or Granny Clampett in a Tinkerbell suit. She skipped as she came toward the table—it was awful.

Weird as it was, we were not inclined to laugh. There is nothing amusing about someone losing their mind. Grandma tossed her beribboned head coquettishly, bantered with the kids and was almost feverishly festive. At one point she accompanied a couple of small girls to the washroom and, holding their hands, she fairly bounced down the aisle, her pink fluffiness as surprisingly inappropriate as a bridesmaid's dress at a wiener roast. It was not funny—it was depressing and sad. We felt sorry for the whole family and quietly wondered how long it would be before she took that long ride on the padded bus.

The two meals progressed, ours quiet and subdued, in the presence of tragedy, theirs quite festive, in what we assumed was a valiant attempt at normalcy. Grandma seemed especially cheerful. She laughed gaily and often, gave the children her undivided attention and seemed genuinely interested in their conversation. She must have been a very nice woman before the bats took over the attic. It was depressing.

The family's check arrived and they gathered their belongings and got up to leave. As they passed our table, one of the moms bent down and whispered a few quick words. "Her eleven-year-old granddaughter made it for Mother's Day." What a revelation! This was not a grandma with a mental problem, this was a Supergrandma who was brave and strong enough to risk her public image out of love for a precious grandchild. Imagine that little girl sweating and slaving to make a beautiful dress for her beloved grandma. Imagine Grandma's mixed emotions when she saw it—about equal parts of pride and horror, I would think.

The WI roll call that made me remember that story was: "Show a favourite handmade gift." I wish that grandma belonged to our group.

A $URFEIT OF EGGS

ON THIS FARM, we have always kept a small flock of chickens. They are a motley crew, crossed and recrossed Leghorns, Rhode Island Reds and Barred Rocks with a strong strain of Araucana. The Araucanas lay lovely aqua, olive green and pale turquoise eggs and are marvellous mothers. Each year we set three or four of the Araucanas and the resulting dozen pullets are our replacement stock. Two years ago something went wrong with the system, a small hatch, too many of the babies were roosters, a larger percentage of old ones reached retirement age, maybe the coyotes got a few. Egg production fell below consumption and something had to be done. We ordered twenty-five pullets.

They were lovely chicks—large, white and healthy. There were actually twenty-seven of them and they all throve. Meanwhile four Araucanas set successfully. We went into winter with the henhouse bulging.

In November the white pullets began to lay and we were delighted with the five or six eggs a day. When the weather turned warm in December, production went to nine or ten and we began sending the occasional dozen to family and friends. By February 15 we were getting fifteen to eighteen white eggs a day and the Araucanas were coming on stream with five or six greens and three or four pinks and browns. As Easter approached, the term "Easter eggs" sounded like a threat. Eggs filled both fridges and I was begging people to take home what they could carry.

Because we have neighbours who sell eggs on a regular basis, I could not in good conscience infringe on their territory and offer our eggs in the neighbourhood. But my friend Betsy had contacts in Calgary who would buy some, a niece took ten dozen and went on a noodle-making binge with her mother-in-law, and my sister-in-law Marie sold dozens to her co-workers. All this was wonderful, but still the eggs poured in—beautiful eggs, huge white ones and large pinks, browns and greens, a pastel bounty that threatened to engulf us. What does one do with that many eggs?

One bakes. A jelly roll takes four large or five medium eggs and bakes in thirteen minutes. If you establish the proper rhythm, you can turn out seven jelly rolls in two hours. The extra twenty-nine minutes are required to cool the pan slightly between cakes. "Jelly roll" is a misnomer, really—my cakes are filled not with jelly but with lemon butter, because a batch of lemon butter uses five eggs. A sponge cake takes five or six eggs, and if you rip up half a sponge cake and add Jell-O and vanilla custard (which uses three eggs) you have a fairly decent trifle. French toast uses a lot of eggs, and a friend gave me a recipe for New Zealand Pavlova, a meringue-and-fruit dessert that uses four eggs. Raisin pie uses lots of eggs, and there are always egg salads, devilled eggs, fried eggs, omelettes and soufflés. If it is true that too many eggs adversely affect cholesterol levels, we are all in trouble.

One Monday night I came to the realization that my preoccupation with eggs was beginning to affect my personality. I took a jelly roll to a meeting and was gratified to see it disappearing, but then people were going home and a three-inch piece remained. A man approached the table, cut a small slice from the remaining cake, wrapped it in a napkin and tucked it into his briefcase. I was so happy to see such appreciation for my egg-laden confection that I pounced on the nice man and, babbling incoherently, I wrapped the remaining cake in plastic and handed it to him.

"No, no," he protested, "I just wanted to take this taste to my wife."

I was not to be dissuaded. I insisted. I thrust the sticky package into his open briefcase.

Now I am sorry. So if the nice man is reading this, please try to understand that I've been under an awful strain with this egg problem. I hope your papers weren't all stuck together, I hope the lemon butter washes out of your briefcase, and if you and your wife en-

joyed the jelly roll, would you consider stopping by for the recipe
and five or six dozen eggs?

Revenge of the Coffee Maker

WE ARE COMMITTED coffee drinkers in this house and I suppose we
have to admit that we are addicted to the bean. The coffee maker
gets a lot of hard use and requires regular cleaning if it is to be at all
efficient. By last weekend it had become terribly noisy, and so slow
that Ralph and I wondered if we should start our morning coffee before we went to bed. I couldn't put it off any longer—the coffee
maker would have to be cleaned.

I ran several batches of vinegar through it and then fresh water
for several more cycles. Everything was perking along nicely now—
the explosive pops and bangs had mellowed to a gentle purr and the
cold water that I fed into the reservoir took only minutes to flow
steamily into the pot. Then I made the mistake of looking at the bottom of the overhang that holds the basket and filter. It was awful
under there. One doesn't think of coffee as being oily, but it is, and
this brown, greasy mess required my immediate attention. I reached
for a paper towel and tipped the machine so that I might reach the
area better. It was then that I remembered that the reservoir was still
full of hot rinse water.

While I was wiping up the counters, floor and stove top, I decided that I might as well do the entire stove as long as I was in the
business. I ran the sink full of hot water and dropped in all the re-
movable parts. The stove is only a few years old and its design is
supposed to be as modern as anything can be. Everything lifts off of
the actual working surface, so there are no nasty places to bail out

when the potatoes boil over and, unlike my old stove, it has no dark interior with wispy bits of insulation where cremated moths may lurk. This is all very nice, but why, when they were designing this lovely cooking surface, did they mount all the control switches on a nasty little dust- and slop-collecting ledge where debris automatically funnels into the innards? And why doesn't the enamel cooking surface fold over the chrome trim instead of meeting it in a long, miserable trench that can only be cleaned with the tip of a paring knife and a corner of your dishcloth? I would like a word or two with the engineer who designed these handy features. And I'd like a sharp stick in my hand while we talk.

Now that the stove and coffee maker were shipshape I decided to wipe out the microwave so that everything would be equally clean. I put a cup of water inside the oven and set the timer for three minutes. The idea is to boil the water and steam up the oven, so that wiping it out is quick and easy. I have done this a hundred times. This time, instead of boiling and steaming nicely, the water sort of erupted and exploded and shot water all over the oven. When I opened the door, water dripped from the screen that covers the fan and seeped under the tray and out the door. I took everything out and cleaned the oven's walls, ceiling, tray and floor. Everything cleaned up beautifully and I was quite pleased until I realized that the light was no longer on. The micro was dead. I called the repairman.

When I had begun cleaning the coffee maker I had emptied its contents into a covered jar, confident that I could heat it in the micro later. Well, that was no longer an option, but I needed the coffee and I needed it now. I poured coffee into a small saucepan and set it over a burner on my gleaming stove. From the cupboard I took one of my favourite glass mugs. The coffee boiled up and began to spit on the spotless stove. I snatched up the kettle and poured boiling liquid into my glass mug. The mug broke.

That is why I am writing these words from my room here at the Sleepy Pines Rest Home, where I am not allowed to go into the kitchen under any circumstances, and I really don't mind.

$\mathcal{M}$OTHER'S DAY

MY MOM, Martha Johnston, passed away at age ninety-four. My husband's mom, Anna Olson, died at almost eighty-five. Together they mothered for about 135 years. I have been a mother for less than a third of that time so I suppose I am an amateur by comparison, but I am a good observer and I have learned a lot from these two very special mothers.

A mother's primary instinct is to mother. From the moment of birth through all of her life, your mother is your mother. No teenager ever thinks that her mother understands her and maybe she doesn't. The truth is that a mother is too close to the subject to make an unbiased appraisal. It helps if you try to remember that she too was young not so long ago and had all the problems, insecurities and fears that you have today.

A mother loves you and often she loves you despite your characteristics, not because of them.

A mother's frame of mind sets the atmosphere of the home, but the father's frame of mind affects the mother's frame of mind.

Mothers are the world's single greatest influence on civilization.

Mothers have a phobia about mitts, coats, sweaters, boots, food and cleanliness. Without conscious thought, a mother can correct your grammar, tell you to wash your hands or sit up straight, ask if you are warm enough and offer food.

A mother worries about your weight problem and makes you doughnuts.

A mother loves all her children equally and has no favourites, unless of course one of them needs her.

A mother is very intelligent when her children are little, downright stupid when they are teenagers. She miraculously smartens up again as her children mature.

Mothers and grandmothers don't buy candy as often as fathers and grandfathers do, but they are pushovers for ice cream, fruit, nuts, yogurt and books.

A mother listens to your memory work and then surprises you by reciting twenty-four verses of *Evangeline*. She also knows all the words to some very old weird songs.

Mothers are wonderful cooks and each one has a specialty—biscuits, bread, meatballs, lemon pie, etc.

A mother is a wife, nurse, chauffeur, hairdresser, laundress, gardener, vet's assistant, decorator, psychologist, cook, maid, seamstress, janitor, secretary, handyman, buyer, accountant and diplomat. She may or may not have an outside job, she does community work and is available to her friends and extended family, and she still finds time to make Halloween costumes, birthday cakes and Christmas cookies.

A mother does not believe that her child ever did anything really rotten. Foolish or thoughtless maybe, but not really rotten.

A mother is afraid that you will not have enough sense to wear good shoes with your new dress when you are forty-six years old.

A mother is equal to any emergency. You know in your heart that should her child be threatened, she can perform surgery, fly a plane or tackle a grizzly.

Mothers take the egg with the broken yolk, the cupcake with the messy icing and the cold pancakes. They also get the first pussy willows, wilted buttercups, fistfuls of dandelions, handmade art objects, secrets, knock-knock jokes, sentimental but sincere greeting cards, and lots and lots of love.

Mothers sit down last.

A girl who has never been mothered is dreadfully handicapped when it comes her turn to mother. A boy who has never been mothered is going to have a hard time forming a close relationship.

Be aware, all you young mothers: the good or evil that you do now goes on into succeeding generations.

Happy Mother's Day.

THE $School BUS
DOESN'T STOP HERE ANY MORE

IN MARCH 1983, when the "Pre-Registration for Grade One" forms came out in the local papers, I began to get this sick feeling. It seemed like a week ago that we had filled out those forms for our first grade one'er and now the third and last was about to graduate.

The sick feeling struck again in April, when Ralph and I realized that we had just attended our last parent–teacher interview, and after that I felt mildly depressed most of the time. The last band concert, last parade, last report card, last basketball game, and finally it was the very last day and the last time the school bus would stop at the end of our lane.

In all those years I don't think we ever missed an open house, a parent–teacher interview, a band concert or an achievement night. We never missed one elementary science fair during the years that our kids were in them and we have seen most of them since. We have gone to every spring concert and I have taken my turn as bus rep and Home & School Member. The School has been a great big part of our lives, we have come to feel a certain sympathy and affection for many of the teachers, and I met several of my favourite people through school associations.

For fifteen years it was not unusual for us to make five trips a week to Cremona and we often made more. Before the kids had driver's licences, it took two trips every Monday to deliver and pick up from the band bus. Every Thursday I picked them up for piano lessons, and there were Explorers, Cubs, Shop Club, basketball, badminton, gym decorating, yearbook meetings and so on. Small wonder our car turned toward Cremona automatically.

Not all of these "lasts" are sad. I hope I have fallen over my last clarinet, I hope never again to have to move three piles of schoolbooks off the deep freeze to get out a loaf of bread, or off the washer to put in a load of blue jeans. I hope I've heard my last tirade on the general rottenness of school bus travel, I hope never again to sit huddled in a dark, cold car, waiting for a band bus when the roads are covered with ice and it's twenty below zero and blowing snow. I hope to spend less time picking up and putting away. I hope my scissors, hairbrush and nail clippers will stay where I left them and I hope Ralph and I have worked on the "last" shop project that should have been turned in "last" Thursday.

But I would miss the band and school newsletters. It was nice to know ahead of time about upcoming events. I knew I would miss the latest news on the school grapevine, the help with meals and dishes, the latest awful jokes, the extra place at the table, and I had a few tears on the first few days that the school bus didn't stop here any more. My goddaughter Kate and my grand-nephew Ryan started school that year. To them and to their mamas, twelve years seemed like forever, but it's only a moment—hang on to it, enjoy it.

The other day I parked near a lady who had five little kids ricocheting off the doors and roof of her station wagon. She was a pleasant-looking young woman, maybe a bit tired, but calm and reasonably happy.

"Are those all your kids?" I asked her.

"Yes," she replied, surprised and bit defensive, probably wondering if I was a mental case.

"You are a lucky woman," I told her. "Enjoy them while you can."

SUMMER

The hummingbird feeder goes up on May 15. Any later than that and a hummer will be buzzing the kitchen window and looking angry. By early June the spinach, planted last fall, is ready to pick and we have the first real summer salad. After that it's a banquet of fresh vegetables every day—radishes, lettuce, green onions, baby carrots . . .

The lawn needs cutting every few days, cows and calves gorge on tender new grass, weeds sprout as fast as we can pull them, the bedding plants have taken root and look good, nasturtiums spill from their containers, the fountain is hooked up in the grotto, and crops are tall enough that the wind transforms a field of barley into a billowing silver-green sea. Wild roses and pink and burgundy dogwood line the ditches. Yellow lady slipper has made a comeback in our area and there are glorious beds of them under fence lines.

Summer is picnics on the lawn, great golden fields of canola, deer eating the rosebuds, family reunions, barbecues, parties, weekend guests, overnight guests, family dinners, and cutting hedges, painting the fence, staking the peonies, taking a precious baby grandson to the lake. Summer is so brief and so wonderful that we can't bear to waste a minute of it. It's our reward for putting up with winter, and we deserve every second that we get.

A DRIVE IN THE COUNTRY

MAYBE TWO OR THREE times a summer, we go for a drive. Sometimes it's a Sunday afternoon drive, sometimes it's an all-day affair and we call it our annual holiday.

My idea of a nice drive is a leisurely tour along peaceful, familiar wooded roads, with frequent stops to observe wildlife, dabble in running water and identify birds and flowers from our bird and wildflower books. I like to take along a spade in case I see a tiny juniper or lungwort or cactus. Once I brought home some sage from near Drumheller and it took two years to become beautiful, two more years to nearly choke one of my flower beds and five more years to completely grub it out.

I like to pick up odd rocks and listen to running water and touch and smell the growing things that are different than the ones we have at home. If I am the driver on one of these outings, we are likely to come to sudden, unexpected halts with me calling sharply, "Look, look, a blue heron!" or "Deer!" or "Yellow-headed blackbird!" etc., etc.

My husband's idea of a nice drive is to find a road we've never seen before, preferably one under construction, and even better one with sharp, crumbly shoulders that overhang dark, bottomless canyons. If the road peters out and we have to turn around on an eight-foot wide piece of soft gravel so that the rear wheels hang out over a precipice, that's part of the challenge. Ralph stops the car at museums, historic sites, occasional point-of-interest signs, and thirty seconds before your bladder bursts. He does not stop for glacier lilies, swans, moose or that bright blue patch of flowers that I don't know the name of. I will spend the rest of my days wondering if those yellow fields near Edson are tall buttercups and if I was right in identifying heart-leafed arnica, while leaning out the car window at 50 km/h.

He frowns upon my digging anything up—"Remember the sage?" He believes unusual rocks are best left in their natural habitat and he says that people who stop along the road and get bashed from behind get just what they deserve.

When I'm driving I can see that he is tense and uneasy, expecting me to stop abruptly in heavy traffic. I hardly ever do. When he is driving I am frustrated and cranky because I know that we are missing lots of beautiful and unusual birds and flowers.

Do I enjoy these outings with my husband? I sure do. I love being with him under any circumstances, and when we are in our nineties I hope I'm still yelling, "Stop dammit, that may have been a whooping crane!"

KEEPING IT *S*IMPLE

ABOUT THE FIRST of May in the year my dad turned eighty, my sisters, Mom and I began reminding each other of his birthday coming up on August 22.

"We'll have it right here in the house," Mom said, "and we'll just have the family."

"Mom," we interjected, "the family now includes fifty-four people and two imminent babies."

"It's at the end of August," she reminded us. "The weather will be nice and some of you can go outside."

In June we said, "Don't do any cooking, Mom, we will bring all the food. And for goodness sake let's keep it simple."

"I'm going to have Laura cater it," she announced. "None of you need bring a thing."

"Laura!" I yelled. "The last time Laura catered a family affair she brought enough food to re-assemble two steers and a hog. I thought we were going to keep it simple—family only, cold plate and birthday cake."

In July, Marj piped up, "When we were counting family we forgot to count Mina and Bob, they plan to be here in August. And how about Auntie Georgia and Dott and her family?"

Mom looked a bit sheepish. "I'd kind of like to ask Mae," she said, "and Vic and Mildred, and how about Marie and Ruth and Helen and Elsie and Vi and Ed and Mabel, and then there's Paul and Hilya."

"We are having the party at our place," I announced. "My kitchen is more convenient, I have more fridge space and the yards are all set up for a picnic anyway."

"Oh good," Mom said, "I was hoping you'd offer. But for goodness sake keep it simple."

The birthday party was a huge success. Everyone came, even Cousin Marlene from Dartmouth. The weather was gorgeous and the yards and gardens had never looked lovelier.

The guest of honour took time from his busy schedule and drove down in his own car. He had to go back that night though—he was building two more wagons, he had people coming to look at a sleigh and there was an order for a breaking cart. He said he'd trim the horses' hooves next trip.

We had enough food for our family, all the extra guests and two Hutterite colonies. We had every type of pie and every kind of salad, we had chili and ham and turkey and dressing, fourteen varieties of pickles and a birthday cake.

Because of Dad's fifteen years in the legislature it was a thrill to have Bob Clark come and present certificates from the Legislative Assembly, Lieutenant-Governor and Premier. Dad was very pleased and gave an acceptance speech that showed his political skills to be as sharp as ever.

The medley of Dad's favourite songs went over pretty well even though the singers were under-rehearsed. Thanks to Ruth Konshuh and Glen Ray we had twenty-two verses of "The Old Chisholm Trail" and all of "Abdul Abulbul Amir." Louis and Myra Hildebrandt served as official photographers, and as a special surprise for

Dad, Clifford Aarsby, a friend from sixty years ago, attended the party.

If I do say so myself, hiring the piper was a stroke of genius. Bill Bagnall found him for us and he was a gem. First we heard the pipes from afar and then, with swirling kilt and skirling pipes, he came round the curve and into the yard. There wasn't a dry eye in the crowd.

"It was a wonderful party," Mom smiled after everyone had gone home. "My, I'm glad we kept it simple."

FLICKER FAMILY FURNISHES FLAT

WHEN WE MOVED to the farm a huge blue spruce dominated the east flower bed about twenty feet from the kitchen window. We enjoyed the tree for about another ten years and then it became a casualty to a May storm in which rain and sleet froze into leaden blobs that ripped out power lines, fences and trees. The top was broken out of the tree, as were several big branches, and gradually the damaged parts dropped needles into the grass and the flower beds. It was a sad day when we admitted that the tree would never really recover and an even sadder one when we actually cut it down.

Pulling a stump that size is going to make an awful mess of a lawn, so we cut it off flat at about three feet and incorporated it into the decor. As the stump dried, the bark loosened and we pulled it away to expose a smooth, silvery surface. Some nicely shaped rocks and a little blue hand pump rest on its sixteen-inch top. Delphiniums, bleeding heart, peonies and yarrow grow nearby and a truly magnificent shelf fungus, big enough to shelter a family of gnomes, grew out near its base. We liked our tree stump, and in spring when I dug the grass from around it and the roots crumbled beneath my spade, I felt a bit sad to think that very soon it would be so unstable that we would have to dispose of it, and then even this stage of its usefulness would be over.

On a Monday in early June we noticed a yellow-shafted flicker examining the stump. The flicker is a pretty impressive citizen of the bird world, 12½ inches long with a brown-barred back, spotted underparts and black crescent bib. Both male and female have a red band across the nape of the neck, a white rump that is most conspicuous in flight and a yellow lining on wings and tail so that when the bird flies in sunlight, or spreads wings and tail to land, you see flashes of gold. The male has a black moustache line that streaks into the side of his throat, and I wish I'd paid better attention to the bird who began boring into our stump because now I don't know whether it was Papa or Mama who actually chose the nest homesite.

Whoever it was, not a moment was wasted. While one bird sent chips flying into the delphiniums, its mate perched nearby and murmured things that roughly translated as, "Bear in mind, Francis, that the furniture comes Thursday," and "Can't you get a higher ceiling than that in the library?" By Monday evening only the tail showed on the working bird, and by Tuesday evening the cavity was large enough that the bird was wholly inside and only great pithy chunks of wood flying out of the hole betrayed its activity. Sometime on Wednesday a slab of the exterior wall fell out, exposing more of the interior than I think they had in mind. But who knows, maybe they are into sunrooms and solar panels. We couldn't see much change by Thursday evening and we wondered if the extra exposure, dog activity and gardeners had discouraged the flickers. We were a bit disappointed that they had gone but not surprised.

Friday morning a glistening white egg lay on the unlined bottom of the nesting cavity.

Ralph and I carefully replaced the fallen slab that may or may not have been part of their sunroom, but we were not terribly hopeful about the future of this family. On Saturday morning, one of the parents emerged from the cavity and flew off into the woods carrying the lovely white egg in its beak.

We hope that the flickers' marriage survived the combined trauma of interior construction, amateur repairmen and having to move when the baby was so small. We hope that the egg was carried to a more secure nest site and that it and its siblings hatched and grew strong.

This summer, when we see a lovely young flicker snatching ants, we are going to assume that he began life in our old tree stump.

CATERING *Chaos*

MY WOMEN'S INSTITUTE would rather not cater at all, but if the occasion is important to one of the members, they do a perfectly beautiful job. The Writer's Workshop was important to me. It was sponsored by the Alberta Summer Games, and Betsy Gentry and I organized it. Betsy did the executive work, contacting the writers Jack Peach and Jan Truss, getting permission to use the library, ordering the wine. I did the easy stuff, like writing up ads, taking forms to the Games office and arranging for the lunch.

Lunch was certainly simple enough. I just asked the WI, and like a well-oiled machine it swung into action. There was one little hitch. According to my research, it happened this way.

Scene 1, Monday. The committee meet under chairperson Elma Bird to plan the menu. Committee members then go home and phone the directors with the list of food assignments. The directors will contact individual members to prepare the dishes. Committee member Lita Reid gets on the phone and talks to director Pearl Stone.

Lita: "Catharine—lemon sauce for twenty. Holly—butter, celery and carrot sticks. Alice—potato salad for twelve—"

Pearl: "Wait a minute. Alice hasn't been well, you know. Couldn't we just skip her this time?"

Lita: "Of course we can. I'm so sorry she's not well. Just leave Alice off the list. I will do her potato salad."

Scene 2, Thursday. A car speeds toward Ponoka, the home of Lita's parents and mine. We are on our bimonthly visit to our folks. Lita and her twin Rita, whom we have met at Innisfail, are in the front seat discussing their forthcoming family reunion. I am in the back seat making notes on a Summer Games assignment and half-listening to the sisters' conversation.

Lita: "I wish Alice's donation had been a cake or something that I could do ahead. With the class reunion and family reunion that same weekend, I will have to do the potato salad at about 4:00 AM."

Noreen: "What's all this, Lita? I have lots of eggs and lots of potatoes and Kirsten [my daughter] will help. Let me do Alice's salad."

Lita: "Oh dear, I wasn't trying to—"

Noreen: "I know you weren't, just let me do it."

Lita: "Well then, let me do your part."

Noreen: "I don't even know yet what I'm bringing. Don't worry about it. I'll do the salad and whatever."

Meanwhile, Holly has stopped by to visit the ailing Alice. Scene 3 takes place in Alice's yard. Holly is standing on the front walk and looking up to where Alice and her husband Bud are shingling the roof. I don't know how Holly knew about the potato salad. The WI has a network all its own.

Holly: "Good grief, Alice, should you be up there? Is this the woman who is too sick to make a potato salad?"

Alice: "I'm feeling much better, thank you, and I intend to make my own salad."

Scenes four to eight are when confusion really sets in. Evelyn phones to say that my assignment was angel food. Lita phones to say that she has already made it. Alice phones to say that she will darn well make her own salad. I phone Lita to say that Alice insists on doing her thing and now I'm making my own cake. Alice phones me to say that if she is making salad anyway she will double it and save me doing anything, as I am up to my ears in registration, floral arrangements and protocol. I begin to wonder if I am confused and should be making potato salad instead of angel food. Whatever it is, I am pretty sure it involves eggs.

The Writer's Workshop was very successful, the featured guests were charming, the setting had the proper ambience, the lunch was lovely, the potato salad was delicious—and the angel food wasn't bad either.

GARDEN *G*URU MILDRED MULCH

MY GUEST COLUMNIST this week is the garden guru, composter and conservationist Mildred Mulch. Miss Mulch is going to answer some commonly asked questions submitted by her faithful readers and fellow gardeners. Miss Mulch's own garden is totally pest- and disease-free, her annuals begin growing the day they are set out, her perennials are lush and laden with blooms, no grass grows past her perfect edges. The few weeds that grow in her garden are easily hand pulled, aphids ignore her lupins and she long ago eliminated chickweed and groundsel from her entire property. Bluebirds and goldfinches sing sweetly in her ornamental shrubs, hummingbirds practise ballet at her feeders, while her lawns and hedges sweep gloriously green to the edge of untouched old-growth forest. Miss Mulch's garden is unfortunately not open to the public, as it exists only in her mind.

Some of the following letters may have been edited for clarity.

Dear Miss Mulch,

The thumb and thumbnail on my sister-in-law's right hand is permanently stained and cracked. She says it's from gardening. Do you think it is safe for her to prepare food? Is this condition contagious?
—L.G.

Dear L.G.,

Your sister-in-law's condition is caused by deadheading petunias and pansies, and it is not contagious. It is safe for her to prepare food but she probably does not have time to do so anyway, so don't worry about it. Why don't you take her a sandwich occasionally?
—M.M.

Dear Miss Mulch,

In a corner of my garden there is a really lovely looking plant that has not yet bloomed. How can I tell if it is a flower or a weed?
—P.G.

Dear P.G.,

Take a firm grip, low on the plant's main stem, and pull. If it breaks off at ground level, leaving nasty tendrils that begin growing even as you watch, it is indeed a weed. If, however, it pulls out nicely, root and all, it was a flower and probably one you have always wanted.
—M.M.

Dear Miss Mulch,

This spring I planted lots and lots of lobelia. Some of it is very nice but a lot of it just died. How can I avoid this problem next year?
—R.J.

Dear R.J.,

All lobelias are born with a death wish. The plants that live are probably very unhappy for having been thwarted from their true calling. Take solace in knowing that the little dried-up brown ones are the truly fulfilled ones. —M.M.

Dear Miss Mulch,

Some of the leaves on my monkshood and globe thistle are sort of folded in and there are worms in there. I also have aphids all over my lupins and they are sticky and awful. Please comment. —W.H.

Dear W.H.,

Two comments come to mind, eeeeww and yuck. —M.M.

Dear Miss Mulch,

I have great difficulty maintaining any kind of gardening program. Can you recommend a schedule or timetable that I might follow? —T.F.

Dear T.F.,

I can only share with you the program that I follow. Walk through your garden and watch for the plant or plants that seem nearest to death. This may be from lack of water, insect infestation, over-crowding or being choked with weeds. Tend this plant first, and by the time you have finished with it, there will be another that is in equally desperate circumstances. When that one has been rescued, there will be another. There is no end. In medicine I think this is called triage. I call it the JAID method, or Just Ahead of Impending Doom. —M.M.

Miss Mulch regrets that she cannot answer more questions today, but she has left her office window open and she can hear some hanging plants making choking sounds, so she has to go and water them.

FATHER'S DAY

MY HUSBAND'S DAD John Olson passed away at age eighty-eight. My dad, Glen Johnston, died at age ninety. Together they totalled more than 130 years of fatherhood. My husband has been a father for forty years. I have been on rather friendly terms with all three of these very special fathers, and from my observations I think I'm qualified to make a few statements on fatherhood.

A father makes a person eat parsnips and liver when she is little, but objects when that same person (made strong by parsnips and liver) stuffs oatmeal into his balky grandchild.

A father brings home McIntosh toffee, Scotch mints, licorice see-gars and maybe humbugs. He does not bring jujubes, After Eights or butter mints. Whatever kind he brings, it's the best-tasting candy in the world.

A father calls you leadfoot and asks about your driver's licence until you are twenty-eight years old. He notices the wear on the inside of your tires, makes sure you get a proper wheel alignment and for some reason becomes absolutely furious when he finds out you've been driving in winter with a faulty heater. He also teaches you to dance, gives you money for the movies when he can't afford to, sets an example, settles disputes, makes final decisions, builds fences, plants potatoes and trees, and can imitate bears, hawks, coyotes and meadowlarks.

A father yells at you for wasting toothpicks and ice cubes, but wouldn't think of denying you a sirloin steak, a quart of milk and half a gallon of ice cream.

A father writes your name on your pancakes in syrup and he can pour your tea from two feet above the cup and never spill a drop.

A father finds the money for things like a piano, ice skates, the dentist and Christmas presents, even if he hasn't had a new suit in fifteen years.

A father has time to plow through mud, ford swollen creeks and wait at the bus depot for eight hours if his kids are coming home, but he doesn't have time to sit around the house when it's twenty-five below.

A father's lap is the absolutely best place to be if you are cold, not feeling well, wrapped in a towel, in trouble, reading comics or just feeling lonely.

Fathers teach you funny verses, terrible jokes and occasional words that might better be forgotten.

Only a father would move twenty-seven hay bales by hand, at night, after a hard day's work, when a kitten that nobody needs has fallen down a crack in the bale stack.

A father is the only one who can make peace between a warring mother and daughter. He is also the only one who can calm a mother who is hysterical over a little mud and a few footprints in the entry, utility room, kitchen and bathroom.

A father can explain the unexplainable, fix the unfixable, forgive the unforgivable and love the unlovely. He catches moths with his bare hands, is not afraid of blood, can't remember where his scars came from and could easily kill a tiger to protect you. But he is reduced to mush by tears in his daughter's eyes.

His very presence in the next room discourages boogeymen, dispels nightmares and makes thunder less thunderous. He never lies, cheats or steals, never has and never will, and he knows that you won't either.

For all this, a father deserves some special consideration. He gets the biggest dish of ice cream, the last piece of pie, quiet when the news is on, first chance at the mail and complete adoration.

Be aware, all you young fathers. The good or evil that you do now goes on into succeeding generations.

Happy Father's Day!

MAKE A *M*ENTAL NOTE SOMEPLACE

SOMEONE ONCE TOLD ME, "Keg & Cleaver is an excellent oven cleaner." I think she meant Arm & Hammer. One fine morning a sportscaster told us that "hockey schools are especially revelant, in these days of strong competition," and on the news the night before, a politician whose company was being investigated said, "The inquiry should be over in a couple of weeks and then my wife and I can get under that black cloud."

A young woman confided that she had told off her husband's buddy by saying, "Your morals are to be desired." Surely she meant "leave much to be desired."

I once heard about a dog that got frightened and "made a beehive for the house," and about a boy who set records in volley-vault. I still don't know if he was in volleyball or pole vault.

At my kids' school, a voice on the intercom once suggested that the students "not conjugate near the exits." Several of the kids moved off down the hall and chanted "I am, you are, he is, je suis, tu es, il est." Something was gained through this. Normally the students wouldn't have conjugated anywhere but in French class.

One day I was carpooling a load of little boys and only half listening to their various conversations when I heard a nine-year-old tell my son, "I'm an inconvenience." Poor little kid, I thought. He probably was just that, but it's not very nice of his folks to point it out to him.

My son picked it up and said, "Donny, do you mean intermediates?"

"Yeah," Donny replied, "that's what I mean, I'm in intermediates." They had been talking about swimming.

A sweet little lady told me that she "described to the *Alberta Authors Bulletin*" because she was interested in writing. I hope she is also interested in a dictionary.

These mistakes slip onto the printed page more often than they should. A recent cattlemen's newsletter pushed the slogan "Beef sounds good." The writer gave examples of other successful agricultural slogans, which included "Get Cracking," "Have Milk Instead" and, to my sorrow, "Show Your Cheddar more Warmpth."

Some writers have trouble with homonyms. I have seen "Of coarse" instead of "of course," "passed time" for "pastime," "peak" for "peek." "Little Elsie peaked through the open door." I can only imagine Elsie with her head coming to a nice sharp point. Does her mother try to disguise the peak with a big generous hair ribbon, or perhaps a toque?

One of my dad's old friends was the all-time champion of verbal confusion. One day when he was building kitchen cupboards, standing on the counter and sanding the upper cabinets, I went into the kitchen and moved the chair that he had been using to climb up and down. "Are you going to leave me harpooned up here?" he asked.

One summer he wanted one of my brothers to help him and assured Dad that he wouldn't put the boy at a man's job: "I just need him for a few little major things."

While he was sharpening a knife on his hand-cranked grindstone, a bolt worked loose and the grindstone leapt free and careened off into the yard. "There," said John, "goes the speed of gravity."

"How was the parade?" someone asked him.

"Pretty far-fetched," he replied.

His questioner was confused. "How do you mean far-fetched?"

"Well," John explained reasonably, "there would be a float or a wagon or something and then a big long wait till the next item, a pretty far fetch between entries, I'd say."

I have several more of these gems and I plan to keep collecting new ones. To make sure I remember them, as they show up I will, as my old boss once told me, "make a mental note someplace."

ONE MORE WAY TO ᛉUIN A PARTY

WE HAVE HAD LOTS of lovely dinners at our house—holiday meals, family reunions, picnics, barbecues and parties for special occasions. We have also had lots of delightful non-family guests, people with humour, intelligence and charm. Unfortunately these two happy circumstances rarely occur on the same day. If there is a way to mess up a dinner party, we can find it.

We have had late guests, unexpected guests, guests that forgot to come, and once we accidentally got the wrong guests. We have had the power go off with a turkey in the oven, and a roasted duck that was so fat that the dogs wouldn't eat it. We have had steaks so rare that the vet could have saved the animal, and steaks that would pass for beef jerky. Once when I tried to barbecue a chicken on the rotisserie, the wind came up and covered it with ash, and then it began to hail. There was that memorable meal when one of the boys told our guests that the meat we were eating was a pet calf named Copper, and the time the raspberry soufflé slid sideways onto the tablecloth. Why go on? It is all so depressing.

One Sunday I decided to call a very nice couple that we have known for some time and invite them out for a day in the country. "This time," I told my family, "nothing is going to go wrong. We will have everything prepared ahead. On Sunday morning we will only need to marinate the steaks, make the salad and set the table. We have fresh peaches for a cobbler, a garden full of beautiful vegetables, and enough briquettes to make a huge fire so that the steaks cook fast and well. There will be no slip-ups."

By 11:00 AM on Sunday everything was proceeding according to plan. The steaks were marinating, the dressing for the Caesar salad was made, the cobbler was in the oven. John had found that eight minutes at 350°F brought his famous croissants to flaky perfection, Kirsten was washing fresh mint to garnish the new potatoes, wine was chilling and I was setting the table with real linen napkins and the good silver. This was going to be a class event.

"That greenfeed is ready," Ralph said, "and I could finish it in two hours. Will that ruin your whole day?"

"No problem," I replied airily. "We will eat at 2:00."

Our guests arrived at 12:30 and were delighted to find that Ralph was baling and Mark running the bale wagon. They had never seen farm machinery working—could they go out to the field and take pictures? John and Kirsten had everything under control in the house so I was more than happy to oblige. I put them in our car and we whipped out to the field. We followed the baler around so that they could see how it worked, and then did the same with the bale wagon. First one, and then the other, took a turn riding in the tractor cab, and then we got back in the car and bumped our way to the fence bordering the pasture so that I could point out the creek, the springs and the big erratic.

"Would you like to see the east quarter that we farm for Ralph's sister?" I asked.

Certainly they would, so we went from field to gravel to pavement and back to gravel, skimmed sloping curves, wove through tree-lined laneways, bounced over ruts in a field access, made great undulating swoops over little bridges, braked sharply here and there to point out saskatoons and hawks. Oh, I was in great form, and we covered almost twenty-five miles and had a lovely fast tour over six or eight types of road surface.

We were back by 2:00, ready to dig in to perfect steaks, perfect croissants, perfect salad. Everything was wonderful. Right? Wrong.

I take full responsibility for this, and I have nothing but sympathy for the lady. To this day I am very, very sorry about her discomfort and embarrassment, and I cannot apologize enough. Thanks to my fun whirlwind tour of the countryside, she was too carsick to eat her dinner.

Someday our luck may change and we may become famous for our successful parties. In the meantime, they can only be described as memorable.

WEDDING WEAR

IN THE SUMMER when two of our children were married, I had a closet full of reasonably respectable and not overly worn clothing, but tradition demanded that I have new dresses for both weddings. Some women would be pleased at the prospect of shopping for two new outfits. I was not. I not only dislike buying new clothes, I'm inclined to get kind of panicky and feverish even at the prospect. For years I made practically every stitch that the kids and I wore, but I don't sew much any more and the last dress I made for myself has yet to see the light of day. What I prefer is catalogue shopping, but for the wedding of one's beloved children, one feels that one should suffer. So I had to seize what feeble courage I could muster and face the shops.

My mom loved clothes. She worked in a very nice dress shop that carried only "good" brands. All the women connected with our family were hopelessly spoiled because Mom knew our likes, dislikes, colours, sizes and styles. If we needed something new, Mom magically produced it and we paid the bill. If necessary she altered the sleeves or hem, let out or took in a seam, and we picked up the finished product at her house. Shopping was that simple. We never stood in our underwear, exposed and vulnerable, while a clerk wearing size four jeans and a tank top that exposed her navel ring offered to "find that in a larger size," and observed that "this style has been very popular with our older ladies."

I know that it has become perfectly acceptable to wear pants to a wedding, but I think I'd rather not. I also know that "mother of the bride or groom" should be in a pastel, especially in spring and summer, but I don't like pastels, and I know that traditionally mothers are a bit frothy on these occasions—lace, beads, feathers and silk roses—but I don't like those things either. I wanted something fairly modest, longish, that hung nicely and was not tight, had elbow-length sleeves and a cheerful colour that was neither too dark nor too pastel. I think I have just described my favorite housecoat.

Because I am a marriage commissioner I have a seen a lot of mother-of-the-bride ensembles, and they are pretty well inter-changeable. Baby blue and pink are probably most common, but there are also ice green, mauve and yellow. Most of them are laden with trim in the same colour. What's wrong with bronze, dark gold or even a print? I own several outfits that I wear to perform wed-dings but they were not suitable for my children's weddings. They are mostly subdued or dark colours that don't draw attention away from the bridal party. Except for the time I wore a beige linen to an outdoor wedding. It had been raining but now it was lovely and warm, and while we waited for the wedding party to get organized, the grandpa ordered a nearby boy to "get the lady a chair." The chair he fetched was an upholstered chrome model with a cracked seat that had retained about a gallon of rainwater. When I got up to begin the ceremony, the whole seat of my beige linen was soaking wet and about twelve shades darker than the rest of the dress. Since it seemed in poor taste to explain this to the assembled family, I just kept quiet and went on with the show. I didn't stay for refreshments.

What I wanted to do that summer was to go to a store and find a clerk like my mother. I would tell her what I wanted and she would nod wisely and begin sorting through a rack of things that were just my size and in colours that I love. She would not confuse me with frothy doodads and sleeveless two-piecers with tops that expose my flabby upper arms, she would not suggest that I try a shorter skirt or gold lamé with bead fringe.

If this wise and wonderful person exists, I didn't find her. The soft green print with the dark green jacket was quite acceptable for Mark's wedding, although the jacket sleeves were a bit shorter than I'd have liked and the dress neckline a bit low. The lightweight cop-per sleeveless number with matching long jacket did fine for Kirsten's wedding on the lawn and was long enough to allow me to go without nylons, but neither dress was exactly what I had in mind.

I haven't had "exactly what I had in mind" since Mom quit working at the dress shop.

VIP IN THE *G*UEST ROOM

I HAVE BEEN an active member of Alberta Women's Institutes for lo, these many years. I can't believe how many years. During this time I have met, come to know, love and admire a multitude of truly excellent people, so I was pleased but not surprised when Elizabeth Rushton, the president of AWI, called and asked if she could stay here on the Monday night before our Tuesday Constituency Conference. "If you are sure it's no trouble," Elizabeth said, and I was happy to reassure her that it was no trouble at all.

And it wasn't, really. Elizabeth is a lovely person, modest and unpretentious. We have known each other for ages and share a sense of humour. But if the president of your organization is going to be a house guest, you are not going to blow the dust off the guest room dresser, open a can of beans, barbecue wieners and make instant coffee. I bought a few special things: croissants for breakfast, wild rice for an extravagant salad, fresh strawberries. Because I was making broccoli cheese soup for our first course and the aforementioned wild rice–chicken–green grape salad and a "bean and corn salad for twelve" to take to the conference, I had a bit of cooking to do and I had a report to give and handicraft items to tag. I also needed to dust, vacuum, wash floors, put away a few stacks of magazines and books, tidy up my knitting and Hardanger projects, wash away the mud swipes that the dog's tail had made on the patio door and scrub off the grease spots that the birds' suet had left on the deck.

I was wiping up the floor in the second bathroom when Ralph stuck his head in and said, "She will never see this room, you know." He was right, but whether or not she would see the room was irrelevant. There are certain standards that a truly devoted WI person upholds, and one of them is that we do not have the president and an unclean bathroom under the same roof.

Well, now that the rest of the house was in order, I would just spruce up the guest room a bit. The dresser in that room had once belonged to my Grandma Mattern. It was finished in a dark, fake wood grain pattern when I got it and I painstakingly stripped and sanded it to the original wood. There seemed to be several kinds of wood, and the varnish brought out tones from blond to sorrel. It's a pretty old thing, and when I removed the dresser scarf I was disappointed to see that the top was quite worn looking.

I checked the time. A good thirty hours until Elizabeth's arrival, and there were a couple of other things I had been meaning to varnish anyway—the end of a cupboard in the utility room and the towel rings in the guest bath. The instructions said that the varnish would dry in twelve to twenty-four hours. I had a whole six hours to spare. For a person who does most things at the last minute, six hours is forever! The varnish smelled quite strong. Almost brought tears to your eyes. I left the guest room window open.

In the morning the varnish was still sticky and the smell still strong. Any towels that I hung on those towel rings would be there forever, and if I put down a dresser scarf it would have to be surgically removed. I still had nine or ten hours and faith in the manufacturers' instructions, but it seemed like a good idea to assist the process. I plugged in the hair dryer and blew on the dresser for a while and then on the towel rings. About once an hour for the rest of the day, I spent ten minutes aiming the hair dryer at my handiwork. Sometimes I felt that I was making progress, but mostly I had to admit that it was hopeless. As Elizabeth's car drove up the lane I covered the dresser top first with Saran Wrap and then with a large cloth.

By Wednesday the dresser was lovely and dry, and except for a couple of tiny wrinkled spots it looked very nice. It should have another coat, I suppose, but not right now. Probably about thirty hours before my next guest arrives.

BRAIN *L*APSE

I KNOW A LADY who is competent, intelligent and well-adjusted. One day she poured coffee for herself and her husband, opened the fridge and set the steaming coffee pot in with the mayonnaise and milk.

A neighbour of ours who is young, bright and busy was making a very special dish that required a can of cranberry sauce, so she jumped in her car and ran into town. When she got to the store she discovered that the case lot sale was on, so she bought $200 worth of canned goods and was home in time to finish fixing lunch. Of course, lunch wasn't quite what she had planned—she had forgotten the cranberries.

There is something therapeutic about homemade chicken soup and it's one dish that would be hard to spoil, but I know a lady who spoiled hers. She boiled the necks and backs for the required time and then fished them out to cool while she prepared the vegetables. Carefully she stripped the meat from the bones and then just as carefully scraped the meat into the dog dish and dumped the bones into the soup.

In this house we often have pancakes on Saturday evenings. One Sunday morning I found a pancake in the dog scraps, but our dog won't eat plain pancakes. I would have to trick her. I had a pot roast going so I decided to dip a spot of gravy onto the pancake. I don't know how I did it, I only know that I used the pancake to lift the kettle lid and that I spooned gravy all over my potholder.

My sister-in-law's mom was shortening a pair of pants. She measured and cut eight inches from one pant leg and then answered the phone. Once again she measured and cut eight inches, same pant leg. Her husband looks awful in pedal pushers.

At a recent Women's Institute conference, the president of the Alberta group noticed me standing there unemployed and asked me if I would please get a parcel from her room. Certainly I would. I hustled right off to do so. Her room number was 110. I stepped into the elevator and pressed the number 1. Nothing happened. I pressed it again and nothing happened. I began to feel claustrophobic. I pressed the button and took three deep breaths. The elevator was broken, I was trapped, I began to panic. Does one scream in these circumstances? What does one scream? *Help!* seems so common and unimaginative. Before I could decide what to scream, the elevator door opened and two ladies stepped in. They punched the number 2, the elevator ascended smoothly and the ladies got off. All that time I had been on the first floor punching the button for the first floor. I walked downstairs one floor, fetched Madame President's parcel and said nothing to her about my narrow escape.

While I'm confessing, I might as well mention the time I stopped the car, got out, opened the gate, got back in the car, drove through, got out, shut the gate, climbed into the car and for ten seconds searched vainly for the steering wheel. I finally realized that I had scrambled into the back seat.

Do you ever find yourself standing in front of the deep freeze wondering whether you have just put something in or planned to take something out? Do you start to tell your husband something and forget what it is? Do you occasionally forget the names of people you have known for years?

Do these things happen because we have too much on our minds? Are they mental lapses? Are there psychological reasons for such misadventures? How early does senility set in?

WAITING AND WORRYING

"SWEETHEART," I said into the phone, "your dad is combining, the Kydds are coming for the afternoon and nobody has time to go and get you. I thought Uncle Howie had arranged for you to ride home with a family from Lethbridge."

Our daughter Kirsten was phoning from Ponoka. The Rifleman's Rodeo was winding down and she wanted us to go and pick her up.

"Fine," she said, in the coldly dramatic tones that only a wounded fourteen-year-old can manage. "I will ride a hundred miles with total strangers who are probably alcoholics and perverts."

Melodrama is always funny, and I was laughing when I answered her, "Uncle Howie and Auntie Gail would never send you off with alcoholics and perverts. Let me know what time you are leaving Grandma's place and I'll meet you in Carstairs in front of the hotel."

According to my calculations, our daughter and the people whose name I had already forgotten should arrive in Carstairs at about 6:30. I did not want to inconvenience these kind, total strangers so I parked in front of the hotel at 6:15. Before long I wished that I had brought something to read; failing that, I scrabbled through my purse for paper and pencil so that I could write. No pencil. I found my nail clippers, though, so I shaped and filed my fingernails. By 6:45 my nails couldn't take any more attention. I slipped off my sandals and surreptitiously clipped my toenails.

By 7:15 I was getting impatient. I imagined them dawdling over root beer at Red Deer. I had been sitting here for an hour now and an irritating pattern had developed. Three groups of pubescent girls walked back and forth along the sidewalk and five cars cruised up and down the street. The girls giggled and screamed and shoved each other into trees, buildings and garbage cans. The car drivers stared straight ahead as if they were bent on some vitally important errand. A very small blond boy driving an old brown Chevy could barely see over the steering wheel; a big old Dodge coughed and stalled every time it rounded a corner, but its pale, serious driver always managed to coax it back to life before it quit coasting and stopped dead.

By 8:00 I was becoming frantic, and when two little boys started throwing rocks at a tanker on the siding, each deep *gong* bored into my brain like an evil omen. I couldn't sit there one more minute. I started the car and jerked my way into a break in the mad parade. I parked by a pay phone and called my house, and one of the boys said, "No, no one has called here."

"Stay by the phone," I told him. "Something awful must have happened. Do not leave the house unless you have a confirmed fire. I will call back in fifteen minutes."

I put a call in to Uncle Howie at Edson. No answer, of course—they wouldn't be home yet. I considered phoning my folks at Ponoka but they wouldn't know anything and they would only worry. I sat in the car and tuned in newscasts. No accident reports, no ten-car pileups on Number 2, no unidentified body of a teenage girl. Dear God, I laughed when she said "alcoholics and perverts"—what kind of a mother am I?

I phoned home again. No answer. What could possibly have taken him away from the phone? I know—the RCMP phoned, Kirsten is dead and John has gone to get his father. I tottered out of the phone booth and leaned against the car. When I could get my shaking hands under control I dialled my number again.

"Hello," John said cautiously.

I fought for control, my teeth chattering. "Where were you? Why didn't you answer the phone?"

"I had to help Dad move the auger," he said apologetically.

"John," I said quietly, "if you leave the phone again before your sister is found, I will strangle you. I am having a complete mental collapse here and the fact that I have only two children left and just threatened to kill one of them proves it. This may be our last communication—I can feel all the blood vessels in my head bursting."

I hung up the phone, got back in the car, drove around the block and parked in front of the hotel. The teen girls had gone home and patrons were strolling into the bar, several of them laughing. I knew that I would never laugh again. It was almost 9:00. I bent my head over the steering wheel and tried to think of something useful to do.

The car door opened. "I'm sorry, Mom, they had a great big motor home, some tube plugged and the motor was overheating if they drove faster than fifteen miles an hour."

The great dark cloud had lifted and I was so filled with joy and gratitude that I wanted to pay for the miracle of her safe return. I would be a better mother, I wouldn't laugh at her when she was melodramatic, and if ever again she was sent to ride with strangers, I would get their names, licence numbers and birth certificates. And the next time I had to wait for someone, I would make sure there was plenty of reading material in the car.

THE FOUR F'S OF DIABETES

ABOUT TWENTY YEARS after my father became diabetic and shortly after my brother Ronny was diagnosed as well, Ronny and I had a little chat.

"Here are the four F's of diabetes," Ronny told me, counting them off on his fingers. One—Female, two—Fat, three—over Forty, and four—in the Family."

"Thank you, dear brother," I told him. "Your information cheers me right up. You realize of course that you have given me about a ninety-eight per cent chance of developing the disease."

"It's something you should know," he insisted. "Something we should all be aware of and watch for."

There wasn't much I could do about Fs one, three and four. Over the years I have worked on two, sporadically and with varying degrees of failure. I lost thirty pounds before we went to Norway and gained back most of it during the trip. I lost twenty before I went to England and because we walked miles every day and were not entertained by the fabulous cooks of Norway, I lost another five while we were there. This gave me such a reassuring sense of security that when I came home I backslid and regained the pounds on my own cooking.

Most diets suggest that you drink lots of water, and that has never been a hardship for me. We have good water here on the farm and we keep a pitcher of ice water in the fridge. One summer I noticed that the pitcher seemed to need refilling more often than usual, and by harvest time I was drinking enough water that I just kept a glass in the fridge next to the pitcher. I also complained bitterly about the time I wasted in the bathroom and threatened to leave my mending basket in there so that on my frequent trips I could be doing something useful. I also found that I couldn't get to sleep at night without having had at least one huge glass of water.

When the cold weather and snow hit in October, I was almost relieved. I didn't have the energy to do fall yard work anyway, and the little cleaning up I finished had been done with minimum enthusiasm and maximum effort. The wheelbarrow had never seemed so cumbersome. When did the rakes and spades get so heavy? And if God wants grass in the flower beds, who am I to say otherwise?

By mid-November I was spending a lot of time sort of leaning on my elbows and insisting that I felt fine, thanks, maybe a bit tired. "Please make a doctor's appointment," said my husband, and I said, "Yes, yes I will." But first I wanted to get a couple of speaking jobs out of the way and do some Christmas shopping and some baking and write some letters and bring some projects up to date and do the Christmas cards and letter and finish some sewing and get my cross stitch framed and wrap some gifts and . . .

Late in November, when our wi group was serving a tea, my vision became blurry. During the next few days the only time that I was not thirsty was when I actually had liquid in my mouth. I drank quarts of water, ginger ale, orange juice, lemonade, coffee, herbal tea, Clamato juice. Nothing helped. I made a doctor's appointment.

If you are planning to spend a week in hospital, I recommend Didsbury. I had great confidence in my doctor, the staff was wonderful, the atmosphere was healing, the library was extensive and the food, even on a diabetic diet, was excellent. I felt better almost immediately.

Ronny phoned when he heard about my condition and we reassured each other that there are worse things than diabetes. There are even some funny things. I thought it was funny when Dr. Ahmad told me I would hear from his lawyer if I ate anything good over Christmas, and I thought it was funny and touching when my husband hovered over me and offered to trade a cup of coffee for my teaspoon of champagne on New Year's Eve. The other guests probably thought I was a recovering alcoholic.

There were even some nice things about it. I realized I might finally lose some weight that would stay lost, I had wonderful support from family and friends, and then there were the Christmas trees. My vision was still just blurred enough that all lights seem to triangle and within every triangle was a shimmer of light. When we drove across the darkened countryside I saw a veritable fairyland of Christmas trees. Coming into the city I saw a display of trees that would take your breath away—the tail lights on the car just ahead were twin trees in glowing red and some lights on the overpass were seven perfect trees all in brightest gold. If you are going to get diabetes, get it in December. The Christmas trees are almost worth it.

COMMUNICATION BREAKDOWN

EVERY ONCE IN A WHILE Ralph and I get some unusual messages on our answering machine—messages that are not meant for us and that are going to cause some large misunderstandings. If we had any idea who the messages were meant for or who had left them, we would try to sort it all out, but as it is there is not much we can do.

One message was from a man with an authoritative voice who explained quite reasonably that if we would begin loading earlier in the day, the truckers would not have to put in for so much overtime. He gave specific times and instructions that seemed to involve a whole fleet of trucks and then he hung up without giving his name. I hate to think what happened when the trucks started pulling in three hours early and there was no one to load them. I imagine there was some serious yelling and swearing. I hope no violence was involved.

Another call was from a lady whose first name may have been Catharine but whose last name was unintelligible. We tried and tried, but we could not even guess it. Catharine was telling someone that the five pairs of pants he or she had left were now hemmed and could be picked up any time. You can imagine all kinds of interesting things here, the five male members of a formal wedding party pacing around a hotel room in their jackets, boxer shorts, socks and patent leather shoes. A couple who have saved all their lives for a Caribbean cruise, bought an all-new wardrobe and now the suitcase sits half-packed, the plane is on the runway and Dad doesn't have any pants. Maybe it's a young woman who is starting her first job, borrowed money from Mom and Dad for decent work clothes and is about to work her first day on the job in her only outfit, which is faded jeans with frayed holes in the knees and seat.

Then again, you don't need a telephone answering machine to have communication breakdowns. My brother Ronny, who lives at Fort Saskatchewan, golfs with his buddies every day on which no blizzard or hurricane occurs. His house is so close to the golf course that he keeps his golf cart in his garage and just has to ride it across the street and through the alley to be on the course. One day after their usual round, they were heading for the clubhouse when one of the group—let's call him Ed—said that he had to go home early for an appointment. The rest of them left their equipment outside and went in for coffee. When they finished and returned to their various carts and bags, Ed's wheeled bag was leaning against Ronny's motorized cart.

"Well, look at that," his cronies declared. "Old Ed has gone off home and forgotten his clubs."

"No problem," Ronny volunteered. "Since he lives only two doors down my street, I'll just take it with me and put it in his garage."

When the real owner—let's call him Steve—discovered his clubs missing and became alarmed, another member volunteered that he had seen Ronny towing them into Ed's garage. Steve, understandably perturbed, strode over to Ed's house. Finding no one home, he yanked open the garage door and liberated his clubs. At this point Ed returned from his appointment and saw Steve stealing his golf clubs. There was enough yelling that Ronny came out on his front deck to see what was causing all the excitement. No one got hurt.

A few weeks later, another of Ronny's golf buddies showed up at his door with an enormous bag of buns. "My wife told me to bring these over here," he said.

"What are we supposed to do with them?" Ronny asked.

His friend shrugged. "I don't know," he said, "she just told me to deliver them. I guess she got a good buy somewhere and wants to share."

There were sixteen dozen buns in the bag, more than Ronny and Jeannette would use in a summer. Jeannette was suspicious. "That's an awful lot of buns," she said. "Are you sure she didn't just want to borrow freezer space?"

"No," Ronny assured her, "he said she got a good buy and wanted to share."

They gave buns to their children, grandchildren and neighbours, they ate buns with every meal, Jeannette made bread pudding and stuffing for roast chicken, until finally the buns were gone. A few days later, the golf friend showed up at the door again. It seems the buns had been a special order for a family reunion scheduled that weekend.

I appreciate that these communication breakdowns can cause all sorts of inconvenience and that given the right circumstances they could even be disastrous, so in all conscience I can't hope that they continue. It would be nice to imagine that modern techniques and improved electronics would eliminate answering-machine mishaps and guarantee that email messages would never go astray. Who knows, maybe that day will come. If and when it does, our lives will lose some great occasions for laughter.

Thank goodness Ronny and his golf buddies can't be computerized.

WHEN WILL THE *Corn* BE READY?

"GOOD GRIEF!" a visitor exclaimed. "Is that your garden?"

"Well, yes," I answered modestly. "We keep saying we are going to cut down, but each spring it's so tempting to put in a bit more of this and that, and I like to try something new occasionally."

'You can't possibly use all that stuff," she said. "Why do you let yourself in for so much work?"

"We use it," I answered defensively. "We couldn't get along without a garden."

"What do you do with all that corn?" she asked.

"We give a lot of it away," I admitted, and she looked at me pityingly.

"Are all those vines pumpkins?" she said incredulously.

"Some of them are zucchini," I told her. "The rest, I admit, are pumpkins, but the seed was so old I felt I had to plant it or throw it away. I didn't expect so many to come up."

"You must eat beet pickles three times a day," she said surveying the beet row.

"Actually, my husband doesn't like pickles," I confessed, "so we use a lot of them as greens."

"If you eat beets for greens, then why do you need all this spinach and Swiss chard?" She was speaking in a kinder tone of voice now, slowly and clearly, as if dealing with a person of limited intelligence.

I began to feel like a person of limited intelligence. I dug the toe of my rubber boot into the black garden earth and mumbled my reply. "Well, uh—we sort of eat the spinach as an early salad, and I'm afraid we waste quite a bit of the chard. I always mean to freeze more of it, but—"

"I'll bet there are fifty cabbages here," she interrupted me. "Surely you could cut back on that?"

"Mom Olson starts our cabbages and she always tells me to throw away the weak ones, but I hate to make the decision as to who lives and who dies, so I plant them all."

She rolled her eyes heavenward. "At least you used some discretion when you planted the potatoes. My folks' patch was twice this size."

"This is not the main patch," I conceded miserably. "There are six more rows beyond the raspberries.

"Look," I cried brightly, trying to distract her from our potato fetish. "Have you ever tried sugar snap peas? You eat them pod and all. They are wonderful in Chinese food."

She picked one grudgingly, examined it and took a small, apprehensive bite. Her eyes lit up and she popped the rest in her mouth and picked another.

"Look at the carrots!" she yelped. "What can you possibly do with that many carrots?"

I shrugged helplessly. I couldn't say that we pickled some—I had just said that we didn't like pickles. And with ten sprawling pumpkin plants, how could I tell her that we prefer carrot to pumpkin pie?

"When did you last eat a really fresh, young carrot?" I asked her. "These are so good that they make the commercial ones taste like cardboard. Cook up a few of these with new peas and kids who don't eat vegetables will ask for refills."

"Let me get a bag." I went on. "You must try some of this leaf lettuce, it's so crisp and sweet it doesn't need dressing."

We filled three bags, because she wanted to try the red Swiss chard and the beet greens and a small cabbage. She asked me to save four pumpkins for her grandchildren. She even went to fetch the spade so that I could dig her some potatoes. I was very grateful.

I was waving goodbye to her when she stopped the car and rolled down the window. Probably one last word about my stupidity and wastefulness, I thought, but she surprised me. Her tone was gentle and conciliatory.

"When will the corn be ready?"

WHAT ᚱEALLY HAPPENED

"CAN YOU REMEMBER," my brother Dale asked, "the true story behind the little red chair? I know that I chopped it up, but didn't I do it because Mom was crying and I thought the chair was what made her feel so sad?"

"You have confused two different stories," I told him, with the authority of the family historian. "You actually chopped up the little red chair because of Dad. Grandma gave us the little chair at a time when we lived in a small house already crowded with children, toys and necessary furniture. Dad used to pretend that he was falling over the little chair. He did it as a joke, but there was some truth in it too. It was just the right size to trip over and there were lots of things we needed worse than an essentially useless, bulky wooden toy."

"So if I chopped up the chair for Dad's sake," Dale said, "Mom must have been crying after I chopped it up, and that's why I associate her sadness with the chair."

"Mom was upset about the chair," I told him, "but the family heirloom that you destroyed for Mom's sake was one of the little monogrammed liqueur glasses that Grandpa made at the glass factory in Norway. It was just after Grandma died, you were about four, Mom was holding the piece of crystal and crying and you just snatched it from her hand and threw it against the wall. You thought you were removing the thing that was giving her such pain."

Dale shook his head. "What did they do to me when I had these wild delusions of guardianship?"

"Nothing really," I told him. "I'm sure Mom felt terrible about both things but everyone realized that your intentions were good. You were a sweet little kid and you had blond hair and blue eyes and looked angelic. The rest of us always said that Mom liked you best."

"What about the time the curtain caught fire?" Dale asked. "That wasn't my fault, was it?"

"No," I admitted reluctantly, "I did that. But I let you take the blame for a couple of days. Mom had gone out to milk the cow and she said, for about the hundredth time, 'keep the lamp away from the curtains, that's a good way for a fire to start.'" I remember thinking, it can't be that easy to set a curtain on fire. I just passed the coal oil lamp under the light cotton curtain and *whoosh*, fire was licking the ceiling. I set the lamp down on the table, grabbed Dad's black Stetson, climbed on a chair and beat out the fire. When Mom came in I was standing there with the smoking hat and I was a hero. I didn't say you did it, but I didn't correct Mom when she assumed you had. It was only for a couple of days, and then I couldn't carry the guilt any longer and I confessed. You hadn't been punished— you were too small—and I was still a hero because I had put out the fire. It worked out nicely all round. We probably needed new curtains anyway."

"What about the violin, then?" he asked. "Did we also need a new violin?"

"No, we didn't need a new violin," I told him, "and really the one we had belonged to Uncle Jack. That story took place before you were born, so you can hardly be blamed for that bit of destruction.

For years and years I thought I had burned the violin, but it seems Marj was responsible for that. You and she must have the same avenging angel gene because she thought she was saving Mom's sanity when she poked the fiddle in the furnace. Same small house, same overcrowding, Allan and Ronny sawing tunelessly on the fiddle, and Mom said something like, 'That thing is going to drive me mad.' When the boys went outside, Marj opened the top of the heater and dropped in the fiddle. It was gone in about three seconds."

Dale asked whether the other kids had done equally awful things.

I considered his question for a moment. "I suppose they did," I admitted, "but remember there were seven of us, we had no TV, no computer or video games, no Internet to cruise, no mall where we could hang out and our school library consisted of three two-foot shelves. We had a party-line telephone so nobody was allowed to hang on the phone for hours. We had wood fires and coal-oil lamps and not much in the way of entertainment. We did pretty well to grow up as unscathed as we did. The truly amazing thing is that Mom and Dad did retain their sanity."

NAVIGATIONALLY CHALLENGED

MY HUSBAND'S SISTER Alice has a disturbing recurring dream. She is walking down a long hallway with a group of friends. The friends turn off and Alice is left alone and facing a maze of corridors that stretch into infinity. All of the corridors look exactly alike and she has no idea which one to take or which way is out.

Alice is a retired school principal and a world traveller, but like me she has no sense of direction and goes into every new situation with a fair chance of getting lost. Neither of us can trust our instincts, and I think that may be why she has the dream.

If my husband, or my dad, were at the bottom of a coal mine they would know which way was south and where lay the shortest route to the surface. If Alice and I were down there, we would either sit quietly and wait for help, or wander off haphazardly blundering into open shafts and underground pools. It is too horrible to contemplate. I hope I haven't given Alice a new nightmare.

Getting lost in a maze of hallways is an ongoing thing with me. When my mom was in hospital in Red Deer I became disoriented and wandered past the same nurse's station about six times. The first couple of times is no big deal, but by the fourth or fifth round the nurse on duty is looking at you strangely and the casual smile you are affecting has frozen to your face. I got lost in the old CPR station in Calgary once. You wouldn't believe the maze of corridors they have under there. Someone who worked in the laundry guided me back to civilization. I also got lost in the House of Commons. A woman from Oregon guessed correctly that I was a tourist and incorrectly that I knew where I was going and she got lost with me. My husband rescued us both.

If Ralph and I are staying at a hotel, he has to watch me or I will take a wrong turn off the elevator and bumble into a party of strangers in the next corridor. I love the University of Calgary Library but I only go there with my friend Betsy. If I went alone I could become hopelessly lost and never be seen again—a sort of Phantom of the Library flitting about among the stacks, trying to appear nonchalant and hoping that the staff doesn't notice that I have been wearing the same outfit for the last five days. The West Edmonton Mall is another killer. I have been there a couple of times and I truly hate it. I imagine myself as a lost and lonely bag lady wandering between the dolphin pool and Bourbon Street. Occasionally I see someone who looks familiar, but I am too embarrassed to admit that I have been lost since 1987 and anyway my family probably has a new life by now and my return would only confuse and upset them. This could be the basis for a new daytime soap!

One summer day my sister-in-law Marie and I made back-to-back appointments with our Calgary ophthalmologist. Marie drove—she has no problem with her directions. The ophthalmologist had moved since Marie's last visit, but Ralph and I had been to his new office so I did know what part of town he was in. We parked the car and began walking. The route did not seem familiar but I thought maybe Marie knew a shortcut. We walked for quite a long time. By now even the area seemed unfamiliar.

"What is that building?" I asked her.

Marie stopped walking. "It's Mewata Armouries. Do you know where you are going?"

"Well, no," I admitted. "I thought I was following you."

Fortunately it was a nice day and we were early for our appointments.

The family worried when Alice and I went to London together, but maybe we had an advantage. Tourists in England are sometimes injured because they expect traffic to move the same way it does at home. Since we had no idea which way we were going we expected nothing. Occasionally we got lost, but people were happy to help us and we had lovely conversations with them and saw things that we may not have seen if we had always been able to follow a plan.

Alice and I will continue to bumble along relying on friends and family for guidance, and the next time we go to the eye doctor Marie will know better than to let me lead.

COLD *W*AR AT THE CAFÉ

FOR THE AVERAGE university student, a summer job and the wages that go with it determine whether or not he or she goes back to school in the fall. Fortunate indeed is the student with a marketable skill. This lucky person is nearly always a boy, because despite feminism, equal rights, laws against sexual discrimination and the concept of equal pay for equal work, on average men make more money than women. Women pay exactly the same amount as men do for things like cars, gas, tires, food, rent, telephone and movies, but it was ever thus. The old double standard applies in areas other than the bedroom.

Even a few years ago girls could register at a "temping" agency and be reasonably assured of some secretarial or office work. But most temporary service agencies have too many people for too few jobs. Student placement centres often offer jobs that consist of ten to twenty hours a week at minimum wage, no benefits. Not enough to pay your rent, let alone eat and save something for fall. If you get a full-time job you cling to it whether you like it or not, and the days are gone when you switched jobs in search of stimulation and fulfillment.

When Kirsten's friend Cam was a science major at the University of Calgary, he was interested in ecology. His job, driving a cab, was somewhat outside his field, but it was a "marketable skill," he worked in Banff where the scenery was lovely, and maybe he could study some flora and fauna in his off-hours. Besides, Banff had lots of interesting shops, lots of young people and cheerful trendy eating places.

Cam's favourite diner had a special cookie plate that they served with coffee. The cookies were baked on the premises and came four to a plate, a nice change from bran muffins and carrot cake.

One afternoon he sat at the counter, ordered his coffee and cookies as usual and snapped open his newspaper. On the stool next to him a nicely dressed man opened his newspaper and sipped a cup of coffee. Cam's order came, coffee in front of him, food to his right.

He tasted his coffee and was deciding which munchie would be first when his neighbour's hand descended and casually removed one of the cookies.

Cam was outraged. In an almost involuntary move to establish ownership, he snatched a cookie from the plate and ate it. The man looked at him oddly but did not speak. Cam chewed conspicuously, cast a menacing glance at the cookie snatcher and returned to his newspaper. He was taking a sip of coffee when the man took the third cookie, and Cam was so amazed by this effrontery that he almost choked. What was wrong with the guy? Did he think that the cookies were some kind of freebies, like peanuts at a bar? The man didn't look hungry or unbalanced or drunk. Cam fixed him with a stare of righteous indignation and with cool deliberation picked up the last cookie and bit into it. The man glanced at the empty plate, finished his coffee, folded his newspaper, removed himself from the stool, paid his bill and left. No word was spoken.

Cam drank his coffee, finished his cookie and seethed. It's tough enough making a living without feeding uninvited and total strangers, and it was deeply insulting and demeaning to have someone just eat off your plate that way. Still irritated and angry, he folded his paper.

And there, inches from his left hand and previously covered by the open newspaper, sat his untouched plate of cookies.

LITTLE *L*OST DOG

REBA WAS A border collie/heeler cross, four years old, black and white with bits of gold on her face and back legs, and a luxuriantly plumed tail. She looked like a wee border collie with the only evidence of her blue heeler heritage in her slightly bowed front legs.

She was a sweet, friendly little dog and we were very fond of her even if she was not useful. She had the attention span and energy of a hummingbird, ran all day, spent hours in the fruitless pursuit of sparrows and barked in response to coyotes, but not when someone came into the yard. She usually came when called but we couldn't depend on it, and if your voice carried even a trace of annoyance, she crawled under the deck or into a bale stack and did not come out. Reba loved kids—big ones, little ones, friends and strangers. If allowed, she would leap six feet or more into your arms, wrap her paws around your neck and give dog kisses. This is not my idea of dog behaviour and I discouraged it, but our daughter was known to come from Calgary, step out of her car and be hit by a dog missile. There was some justice in this because it was Kirsten who taught Reba the Flying Wallenda trick in the first place, and if her clean clothes got covered in dog tracks, she had only herself to blame.

Reba wanted to be a cattle dog. She could spend hours quietly rearranging a pen full of heifers, and in her puppyhood she herded some chickens to the brink of death. She didn't bite them, she just wore them out. We too wanted Reba to be a cattle dog, but she was a wimp. At the first sign of training or discipline, no matter how gentle, Reba retreated to one of her hiding places and refused to come out. She kept the cats away from the house, she was a wonderfully efficient gopher killer, she didn't dig up flower beds, she could shake hands and sit (though she didn't stay), and if you said to her, "Poor little dog, poor little Reba, are you so sad?" she wrapped her muzzle in her front paw and seemed to cry. Probably most important, she gave and received a lot of love and was delighted to see any of us come home whether we had been gone five minutes or two years. Reba was part of the family and we were very fond of her.

The Cremona Hot Air Balloon Festival was held on a lovely, bright calm Saturday. Seven balloons drifted near enough that we could read their names and numbers, hear the roar of their burners, see the flash of their fire. Ralph and I watched them until they were out of sight. Just as the balloons drifted away over the horizon, our son Mark drove into the yard—but no furry friend ran to greet him. "Where is the dog?" he asked, and we couldn't answer him. We only knew that she had been with us very recently. We checked her doghouse and under the deck, we called and whistled but there was no response. "Maybe she followed the balloons," Ralph said. "Maybe she thought she had finally spotted a bird that moved slowly enough to give her a fighting chance."

When she hadn't shown up by lunchtime, we got in the truck and made a small tour of the countryside, paying special attention to the balloon route. We watched ditches too, hoping that we would not find a crumpled little black and white body. Back home we phoned all the near neighbours and a few along the balloons' path. No one had seen Reba. On Sunday morning I opened the door, hoping foolishly that I would see her bright little face all eager to start the day. No Reba. We made more phone calls, drove farther, checked more ditches, called and whistled. On Monday Ralph walked through pastures and checked anything remotely suspicious. On Tuesday he took apart the bale stack that she sometimes sleeps in. By this time neighbous were calling us.Had we found her? Had we tried the dogcatcher? Their dogs had been frightened by the balloons.

By Wednesday we had almost given up. "Let's make a couple more calls farther west," Ralph suggested, "then we will know that we have done all we can."

Our first call was to a school bus driver just back from her route. "There was a little dog like that at Kinches," she said, "and it looked sort of lost and confused."

Kinches live three miles straight west of us and in a path away from the balloons. Ralph was hardly out of the truck when Reba came trotting out from behind their house. She was happy enough to see us but the Kinch kids, Stacey and Travis, had been treating her very well and she was certainly no worse for her experience. She had been there since Saturday and we have to assume that she had been frightened by the balloons and had run, then became disoriented and finally lost. She was very lucky to come upon a family that treated her so kindly and we are grateful to them.

"What about those stories where dogs come home through five hundred miles of bogs, mountains and blizzards." Ralph wondered. "How come ours gets lost within three miles?"

So it wasn't *The Incredible Journey*. We were still glad to have her home.

THE CLASSIC BARBECUE

THE SUN IS SHINING, the sky is blue, birds are singing in the newly leafed trees and the smell of barbecue hangs in the soft summer air.

That first barbecue of summer—a Caesar salad perked up with a few leaves of volunteer spinach from the garden, butter-yellow potato salad (thanks to the dark-yolked eggs from our free-range chickens), garlic bread, big sizzling steaks basted with our favourite sauce and still pink in the middle, strawberries for dessert. Sounds wonderful, but as is so often the case, anticipation exceeds reality.

First of all, there is not the slightest hope that the grill will be clean. By the time it has cooled down, the rest of the dishes are done and, "Oh, just put the cover on it and go to bed." This means that about the time you begin marinating the steaks, you should deposit the barbecue racks in the utility room sink and spray them with oven cleaner. The sink, your hands and the utility room will grow very messy and smelly. If you wish to avoid this step, you can clean the grill with a wire brush that removes burned-on bits from the centre rods and much of the skin from your fingertips but has little effect on the nasty little corners and overall grease deposit. A simpler way is to spray a little oven cleaner into your marinade. This makes the steaks smell of oven cleaner and your guests will assume that the grill was freshly cleaned. I clean all the little dials and switches maybe twice in a season—it is impossible to do them well and they are messed up again in minutes anyway. Does anybody ever clean the little window inside the hood? Why is it there? It was covered in smoke from the first minute of the first barbecue so no one can look in, and if anybody is looking out I don't want to know about it.

For a classic Alberta barbecue one requires beef, and we have grilled a lot of beefsteak. Some of it has been excellent, a lot of it has been merely edible. We have eaten it in conditions all the way from "Does anyone here wish to re-sole their workboots?" to "If we rush mine to the vet, I think it can still be saved." We have prepared six-pound roasts so that only two pounds were fit to eat, made hockey pucks out of hamburger patties and made pork ribs so tough that you couldn't tell where the meat left off and the bone began. We have dropped wienies through the grill and onto the hot coals, set smokies on fire and made garlic bread into charcoal.

Barbecue cookbooks abound, and according to them the possibilities are endless. There are recipes for satay, shish kebab, chicken wings and bread. Fruit can be grilled to perfection (I'll bet) and the typical vegetable recipe has a paragraph that begins: "Wrap in a double thickness of buttered foil." Foil is a prime ingredient in barbecue cookery, as is sauce, which seems to have ethnic overtones. Add extra cayenne and regular sauce becomes Cajun sauce, lots of tomato and chili and it's Creole, pineapple and ginger for Maui, oregano for Italian. I wonder about carrying this further and throwing in a cupful of salsa and calling it Mexican, nutmeg and cardamom for Norwegian, peppercorns and sauerkraut for German, paprika for Hungarian, or baste with chicken soup and it's Jewish.

Our first barbecue was a little briquette-burning basin on a tripod. The family outgrew it at about the time that the basin burned through. Barbecue number two was half a barrel cut lengthwise, welded to sturdy legs and covered with a piece of crusher screen. We could cook for any number of people on this model, but like all charcoal burners it was hard to light and ate briquettes at an alarming rate. Our current model uses propane and is easily lit, but one lives with the uncertainty of how much propane remains in the tank. There is a rule somewhere that the propane only runs out when you are cooking for company. We have friends who finished off the meat with a blowtorch when this happened to them.

And so we continue to barbecue, not because we are good at it and not because it saves one moment of preparation or cleaning. We barbecue because by living through the winter we earned the privilege, and we Westerners take our privileges seriously. Bring on the oven cleaner and the marinade, break out the baked beans and the coleslaw, fire up the . . .

What do you mean the propane tank is empty?

AUTUMN

From the 20th to the 25th of August, the humming-birds are in a feeding frenzy, and then on the 26th or 27th they are gone. In a state of mild depression I take down the feeder and wash it for the last time this season. A few days later I realize that I can smell fall. The leaves on the trees smell faintly of dust, my husband's clothes smell like ripe hay, the morning air is crisp and sweet, ripening crabapples smell delicious.

Fields of barley still billow in the wind but now the waves are golden. Mouse-hunting hawks perch on huge, round hay bales and long, fat swaths of canola, oats and peas lie in the fields waiting to eaten by combines. A flock of low-flying geese goes over and we can hear them discussing travel plans.

Dig the potatoes and carrots, pick and freeze the saskatoons, make beet pickles and crabapple jelly and raspberry jam. Prepare the garden for winter, make special meals for the men who are bringing in the harvest. If it feels like frost, we take all the hanging and potted plants into the house so that we might enjoy the flowers for just a few more days. The corn is ready all at once. We eat corn with every meal and send some home with guests.

By mid-October the nights are too cold to heat the greenhouse and we bring in the tomatoes. Boxes of them. The leggy plants did pretty well. As usual there are more pumpkins and squash than we need, so we give away a lot. We wean the calves and dig the gladiolas, haul bales into the feed yard. If fall lasted forever we would still find things to do "before winter sets in."

Sometimes the fall is long and lovely with warm days and glorious colour. Sometimes it's short and brutish and ruins the crops. Fall is unpredictable in Alberta.

TRADITIONS — THE *G*LUE THAT BINDS

IF TRADITION IS THE GLUE that binds a family together, then my family must be inextricably bound. We have more traditions than I could begin to list—family sayings, jokes, stories, catchwords, celebrations, pet names and of course food. My mom made the best baking powder biscuits in the world and she was also famous for her pancakes, dill pickles, cornstarch puddings, lemon pies, buns and carrot cake. Dad always said he taught her everything she knew about cooking, and that too became a family tradition.

One Sunday afternoon my sister Donna and I were cleaning up after the traditional roast beef dinner when Donna's six-year-old daughter Kate burst into the kitchen.

"Guess what I found in the barn by the kittens' box? A whole bunch of eggs, maybe ten or fifteen of them."

"Is there a mother hen sitting on them?" I asked.

"No," Kate answered. "In fact, they are cold, so I guess if there are babies in them they are all dead."

"Oh yuck," Donna contributed. "They will all have to be thrown away."

"Wait a minute," I said. "The nest can't have been there for more than a few days, and there may have been two or three hens using it. Let's check the eggs first and if they are good we will make a from-scratch angel food cake. That's what Mom always did when we were kids and found a hidden nest."

Even as I said it I felt a twinge of unease. Mom had a phobia about eggs—she insisted that the little twist of albumen that holds the yolk in place was a germ, and though I told her two hundred times that the little twist was harmless, she still removed it from every egg she used. Would Mom use eggs of doubtful background? Somehow it didn't seem likely, but I was sure that she would have made an angel food from these bonus eggs. It was a family tradition.

Kate brought the eggs to the house. There were ten of them and they were clean and cool. I hadn't made a from-scratch angel food in years; I found several recipes but couldn't remember which of them I liked best. We didn't have any cake flour so I dispatched one of my sons to borrow some from my baking friend Sheila. I cautiously broke one egg at a time and found them fresh and sweet. The whites whipped up beautifully and the kids watched as I whipped, folded and scraped. The cake rose perfectly, smelled fantastic and looked gorgeous. We iced it with a thin, lemony glaze and eight people ate the whole thing after supper. Everyone said it was the most delicious cake ever made and Kate spent the rest of the week looking for hidden nests so that we could make another "angel food like Grandma used to make." The dogs enjoyed the yolks.

I felt very virtuous. Not only had I used the eggs that might have been wasted, I had shown the family how to make an angel food properly and, most important, I had preserved a bit of our pioneer beginnings. I imagined my kids and my sister's children saying someday, "Remember when we found the eggs and made an angel food like Grandma did in the olden days?"

On my next visit to my Mom's I told her all about it. I expected her to smile and nod knowingly, perhaps even recall her mother making some special treat from an unexpected largesse of eggs. She didn't do any of these things.

"Not me," she said. "I didn't make angel foods in those days, and you know how I am about eggs—I can hardly stand to use them right out of the fridge. If I ever found any of doubtful quality I'd have thrown them away."

Well, so much for old family traditions. I wonder how many of the others I am mistaken about? Maybe it was my husband's mother who made angel foods, or maybe I read it somewhere.

Running the Combine

JULIEN, MY HUSBAND'S brother, was here for part of the harvest last year; and of course until school started the kids were able to help, but Julien had to go home to Ottawa, the kids started university and the crew dwindled to one farmer and one unskilled labourer. It speaks well for the strength of our marriage that the farmer and his unskilled assistant still occupy the same bed.

It started out friendly enough. Ralph let me run the combine because the cab is air conditioned and because I don't back up well with the big truck. He made one round with me and explained the power takeoff, the correct gear to use, how to stop and start the elevators and augers and at what height to maintain the pickup.

"It's all pretty simple and straightforward," he said, and (these are his exact words), "Watch that the grain auger is working, that floppy thing is going round and round and stuff is coming out the back."

He drove off to a distant granary. I moved all the proper levers and the combine roared into action. I watched the grain auger, the floppy thing and the stuff coming out the back. I watched so closely that several times I nearly missed picking up the swath and then I came to a corner and had to concentrate all my efforts on that. When the corner was safely negotiated, I checked the auger, the floppy thing and stuff coming out the back. They seemed fine, but what was this tremendous heap of swath tumbling and growing ahead of the table? And why were all the little wheels and belts chattering so horribly, like two thousand sets of those wind-up false teeth? It was terrible. I shut off everything and sat there shaking.

"You have plugged the auger!" Ralph yelled. "When you saw it starting to pile up, why didn't you stop?"

"You didn't tell me I had to watch this end too," I yelled back.

"I shouldn't have to tell you every little thing."

"If it's such a little thing, then why are you having such a big fit?"

The next few rounds were uneventful, then another funny noise began to bother me. It was not a chattering teeth sound, it was a grinding, pounding sound, but the auger was working, the floppy thing flopping, stuff coming out the back and no big piles in front of the pickup. Oh no, the pickup! It was dragging terribly, and clods of dirt were being swallowed by the big corkscrew thing. I hit the lever and the whole table rose about nine feet in the air. I missed fifteen feet of swath, hit the lever again and resumed plowing, overcorrected and rose above the swath. I stopped the machine and adjusted the table height.

"I don't know why I didn't think of this myself," my husband said through clenched teeth. "Fall plowing and combining in one operation."

Late one night as we sat together over corned beef sandwiches and tea, he forgave me for plugging the machine and for ruining the pickup belt.

"Explain to me about the twenty feet of swath you missed in the southwest corner," he said.

"There was a mother grouse in there who must have had a late hatch. The babies couldn't run very fast and I think they were hiding in that piece of swath."

He nodded understandingly. "And how about the big piece on top of the hill?"

"Did you know that you can see the mountains from up there? When the sun shines through the clouds and individual beams fan out onto the mountains, I almost expect to hear a pronouncement from God. I'm afraid I was imagining what the pronouncement might be and I got off track a little. I meant to go back for it, but I couldn't find it."

"Ah yes," he sighed. "That explains the aimless wandering, which was going to be my next question."

"Actually," I told him, "I thought everything went very well. During that whole time, the auger worked, the floppy thing flopped and a lot of stuff came out the back."

Hatsue

WHEN WE APPLIED for a Japanese exchange student we thought we would learn something about Japan, teach her something about Canada and assist her in learning English. We got a lot more than we expected.

According to our advance information, Hatsue Inui was a sixteen-year-old girl whose interests were cooking, hiking and piano. There was no mention of weightlifting, gold smuggling or rock collecting, so we couldn't imagine why her suitcase was so terribly heavy. It was an average-sized suitcase but our above-average men could barely heft it.

Hatsue had come prepared to cook. The suitcase contained food: miso soup paste, spice soup concentrate, several kinds of seaweed, a variety of spices, two kinds of Japanese spaghetti, vinegar, soy sauce, candy, cookies, crackers, instant noodles, green tea and sweet bean dessert, a sort of Japanese Turkish delight made from bean curd. The suitcase seemed bottomless, holding origami paper, T-shirts, a tiny wedding doll, a pair of wooden babies not much bigger than rice grains, photos, fans, newspapers, postcards, ornaments, games, calligraphy paper, brushes and weights and six pairs of chopsticks.

When she wasn't bringing forth treasures from her suitcase she performed magic with things at hand. Cranes from gold margarine wrappers, hats and noisemakers from newspaper, corn soup, Japanese potato salad, sesame beans and coffee jelly from our ingredients and her mother's recipes. Everything had to be beautiful: rabbits made from quartered apples crouched in the salad, two perfect raspberries still attached to stems and leaves finished a fruit salad, cookies in a tin assumed the shape of a giant chrysanthemum.

All was not perfect of course—she was, after all, only sixteen years old. The orange-raisin cake became a baked pudding, delicious even if accidental, and the cream puffs were tasty even if a bit less puffed than she had hoped. She ran the lawn mower over the dog's rug. We are thankful that she and the mower survived—the mat was a wreck. She spilled a pan of unbaked chocolate chip cookies from the pan into the hot oven. We snatched them out as fast as we could but they looked a bit worn, and when they were baked the melted chips made streaks and blots on the cookies. "Interesting design," said Hatsue.

I have always loved Japanese flower arrangements and I hoped that Hats would demonstrate the art. When the wind blew a twig from the apple tree, Hats put the twig and its two apples in a cup of water, and when I pulled a stray cosmos from the corn row she brought in the wilted, droopy flowers and put them in water.

"Honey," I told her, "you can go to the garden and get all the lovely fresh flowers you want."

"But these are poor," she explained. "Their heads are down."

While Ralph and Kirsten baled hay, Hats and I shelled peas, talked and sang nursery rhymes to practise her pronunciation. When she fell off the horse she climbed back on and told Kirsten, "I am Japanese cowboy, Humpty Dumpty."

Hats often confused "if possible" with "if necessary." "If necessary," she said, "and if you would allow, I would sew a simple blouse." Twice the casing went awry and she picked it out. "Do you want me to do it for you?" I asked. "No thank you," she smiled sweetly, "this time sure success."

Thank you, Hats, for wearing your national costume and serving the cake at Grandfather's birthday, for sharing your music and charming our friends and relatives, for "picking up" a million peas, beans and raspberries. Thanks for cooking and baking and cleaning up, for mowing lawns and pulling thistles. Thank you for sharing with us your delight in the hummingbirds, the yellow canola, the vast greenness of our countryside, the garden, the animals and various trips around Alberta. Thank you for your courtesy, good manners, sweetness, warmth and love. You have become a permanent part of our lives.

We said goodbye to Hatsue at the airport on a Wednesday morning, eight weeks later. It was a sad parting but we were all brave and full of promises to write soon and visit again. That night she phoned from Vancouver. "I want to hear your voice one more time," she said, "but I am crying."

Oh Hats, I am crying too.

GETTING READY FOR WI

WHEN A RECENT Women's Institute meeting was scheduled to take place at my house, I admit we made some extra preparations. My sister-in-law Marie washed and polished all the pictures and ornaments and I used the occasion as an excuse to do windows, clean light fixtures and wipe down the bathroom walls. But I didn't go completely nuts and paint the walls, get the carpets and furniture cleaned and buy new drapes. Maybe I have finally overcome my youthful insecurities, or maybe I'm getting lazy, or maybe I'm getting old!

The first time I hosted a WI meeting I made all new curtains, painted every room on the ground floor, got new lino in the dining room and went on a huge cleaning binge, exhausting myself and making life miserable for my husband, kids and dog. Late one night I was upstairs washing windows in an unused storeroom when my husband found me, removed my reddened hands from the hot suds and led me back to sanity.

Two years later it was my turn to have WI again and I launched into the usual cleaning extravaganza, including sending the two big rugs from the living room to the cleaners. Some piece of equipment broke down at the plant and I didn't get the rugs back. I was mortified, but the meeting proceeded and the absence of rugs didn't seem to affect it seriously. On another WI day we had a power failure, so the pump didn't run and the electric coffee perk didn't perk. In desperation I considered offering everyone a pinch of dry coffee to tuck into their lip like tobacco, but the power came on before we had to resort to anything so indelicate. These minor disasters did serve a purpose—I no longer become a nervous wreck over taking my turn at a meeting.

But I still do lots of preparation. I can't imagine how anyone could forget that they were having a WI meeting. The schedules are made up a year in advance and if twenty of your friends and neighbours were dressing up, bringing food and coming for the afternoon, wouldn't that stick in your mind? Wouldn't you have made a note of it somewhere?

A very nice lady who no longer lives in this area did just that—forgot. We arrived at her house one warm September afternoon to find her out on the porch, up to her elbows in unshelled peas. In the utility room behind her the washer was chugging its way through heaps of grubby clothes. The remains of a big family dinner were still on the table, the sink was full of dishes and the kitchen counters were loaded with canning and pickling supplies. She took it pretty well and the meeting proceeded as planned. I would have smiled sweetly, set aside my pail of pea pods and moved to Venezuela under an assumed name.

One doesn't expect much in the way of wildlife at a WI meeting. There is a lot of laughter, but it is not wild. Imagine the meeting in which we had a mouse in attendance. Some people said it was their liveliest meeting ever and several women performed amazing acrobatic feats. Others were perfectly calm—after all, farm women have seen mice—but I'll bet it was a dark day for the hostess.

A former provincial president tells the story of the first meeting held at her house. She was still a bride and anxious to make a good impression on her friends and neighbours, so early in the day she set out to get her outside world in order so that she might devote the rest of the morning to polishing up the house, setting out her pretty wedding-gift china, having a nice bath and doing her hair. Her husband had obligingly offered to "get right out of the way" and go to his folks' for lunch. She looked forward to this time for herself, but first she would just make sure that the two hundred baby chicks in the brooder house had lots of water. Cute little baby chicks, noisy and dusty and smelly but cute. She filled the waterers, turned to leave and found that the door had blown shut. It latched from the outside and it was a good sturdy door.

They found her there when they came to the meeting. She was sitting on the brooder house floor surrounded by chickens. Tears had cut paths through the feathers and dust on her face.

Makes my power failure story sound sort of feeble, doesn't it?

DON'T MAKE FRIENDS
WITH YOUR FOOD

IN THESE TRYING economic times we need all the breaks to keep our families fed and clothed. Farmers have some advantages—we can grow and freeze lots of vegetables, make jelly and jam from our own fruit, keep some chickens and milk a cow, as we did for twenty years. Our city friends think we also get free meat, but we certainly do not. Every animal we eat is one fewer that we can sell and that much less in the cattle cheque. We could probably save money by buying our meat at the grocery store if we got cheaper cuts and watched for specials. However, we believe that first-class food is one of the advantages of being a producer so we continue to eat lots of high-grade beef.

This sounds simple enough—grow and eat your own meat and vegetables. But there's many a slip twixt the cup and the lip. My husband and I really aren't tough enough to be farmers. We don't enjoy seeing our big, tame, trusting steers go to market and certain death, and we fervently dislike choosing one to go off to the butcher.

Never, never make friends with your food. It can only lead to trouble.

Several years ago Ralph and I had to assist a small cow in the delivery of a very large calf. During the birth, one of the calf's hips became dislocated. She was a beautiful, big calf, a warm brown colour with a brockle face. I suppose because we felt guilty about injuring her we gave her special attention. And because she didn't move as quickly as the others, she responded to petting and extra chop, and she became almost a pet.

The calf thrived but always favoured that hip. We were afraid to keep her to maturity for fear that the added weight would complicate her problem. When she was about a year and half old, we decided very reluctantly that the only thing to do was have her butchered.

"Is this your own beef?" a visitor asked, taking a third helping of veal parmesan.

"Yes it is," I said proudly.

"How do you decide which animal to butcher?" he inquired.

"We take a late calf that isn't ready when the others are," I replied, "or sometimes a smallish heifer that's not going to grow out as well as the others."

"Mom," one of the boys interrupted, "isn't this little Copper?"

"Uh—yes," I answered, trying frantically to think of a way to turn the topic.

"Well, Mom," he continued before I could stop him, "wasn't little Copper a cripple?"

The guest's fork froze in mid-air.

"She wasn't exactly a cripple," I said desperately. "She just had a bad hip." I stopped there, believing that a discussion of Copper's birth problems would not save the situation.

"Here," I said. "Have some crabapple pickles, these are our own apples."

The guest was now picking at his salad. "My folks have an apple tree in Ottawa," he said weakly, "but they don't use the apples, they have a problem with worms."

"We don't have any apple worms," blurted the same irrepressible, horrible kid. "But we sure get lots of slugs in the lettuce."

Our guest had only eaten half his salad but at this point he gave up and laid down his fork for good. Funny, he has never been here for a meal since.

TAKING THE *F*ALL

I FALL DOWN A LOT. In fact I consider it my duty to do so, as nothing brightens up an onlooker's day like seeing a fat lady step on a patch of ice and fall flat on her face. Are you expecting a rather sober friend to pick you up for a meeting? Try running out your door, stepping on an ice hummock and falling spreadeagled against her car. She'll laugh! She'll be concerned for your welfare, but mostly she'll laugh. Best laugh she's had all winter.

When your women's group is serving a wedding reception, pick up a big tray of individual salads, back out of the kitchen door and step on a strawberry. The ensuing excitement will remain in the memory of the bridal party long after they have forgotten who made the toast to the bride or what he said.

Once when a cow escaped, I was called upon to help ease her back through the gate, into the pasture. My post was immediately in front of the house, and while backing into an advantageous position, I tripped on the stones in the firepit. In a flurry of ashes, dust and flailing arms, I fell into the charcoal. A fall to remember. And did my family laugh? Three guesses. For weeks afterward, the timing of other events was reckoned by before and after Mommy fell into the firepit. "Did swimming lessons start after Mommy fell into the firepit?" "You did so eat the last cupcake, you had it in your hand when Mommy fell in the firepit."

My little daughter accepted my tendency to fall equably. "I'd race you to the garage, Mommy, but you'd probably fall down and break both your legs."

A small creek runs through our farm and the first summer I lived here, my sister-in-law Jeannette, her two small kids, my five-month-old baby and I set out to cross the creek and take coffee to the hayfield. The baby and the lunch were transported in an elderly carriage. When we reached the creek my little niece Laverne refused to cross. The stepping stones were too far apart; the edges were too muddy; she was scared. I carried her across and my sister-in-law followed; she slipped off the first stone and tracked mud on all the succeeding ones. On each of my three subsequent trips to transport the carriage top, carriage wheels and baby, I slipped on the muddy stones and fell in. Thankfully I did not drown the baby. On the return trip, I ignored the stones and waded the creek. I had to burn my shoes.

All farm wives know what corrals are like in spring. As the sun warms the black, well-trodden earth, an almost liquid top layer forms over a frozen, very slippery bottom layer. I try to avoid the corrals completely then, but there are times when I must help to sort heifers from steers or cows from calves, or administer medicine, or assist a birth. So, unwillingly and apprehensively, I don boots and my oldest clothes and go to my fate. I try to avoid the ice under the sludge, I try to stay on higher ground, I try not to step out of my boots, I try not to fall down. Sometimes I succeed. After one such session I was about to return to the house when my husband said, "Thanks, honey."

"For what?" I asked bitterly.

"Well," he replied, "for those nice smooth spots you left in the corral."

LOST *W*AX AND BABBITT

THE LAST TIME we cleaned out the attic, we came across a box of kids' shop projects. John's little wooden tray shaped like an artist's palette and still sticky after eight years—it must have been boiled in oil before it was varnished. Two really ugly ceramic pots, a pair of metal candle holders guaranteed to scrape the finish off even an Arborite table and, most useless and mysterious of all, a glob of lead mounted on a tiny varnished stump.

The kids' Uncle Julien and Aunt Lilian happened to be visiting us and they expressed some curiosity as to the possible uses of such an article.

"I'm sure it has great artistic merit," Julien said kindly.

"Maybe it has some hidden meaning," Lilian suggested.

"Actually," said Mark, who had been the artist in this case, "an eagle once rested upon this stump, and when he flew away he left this political statement which through the miracle of modern technology we have preserved for mankind."

"It was an exercise in the lost wax technique," I told them. "Dig down a bit and you will find another petrified bird poop that Ralph and I made when Kirsten took that class."

It was a Saturday morning and I was sorting clothes for the wash while Kirsten, who was in grade seven at the time, hovered directly behind my right elbow. I finally realized that she wanted my attention.

"Do you have a problem?" I asked her.

"I guess so," she said. "Mr. Easy says I have to have a project done by Monday or I fail shop."

"What's the matter with you?" I asked. "Why have you let it go till now?"

"I tried to do it," she said desperately. "In fact I tried about five times but something always went wrong."

"Dad and I will help," I soothed her. "Just tell me what the project is."

"It's the lost wax technique," she told me. "You melt some candle wax and drop it into a container of snow to see what an interesting shape it makes."

"Sounds simple enough," I said.

"Wait a minute. Then you put the wax glob into a plaster of Paris mould and melt out the wax."

"Maybe I could get some clay from Marguerite Krebs' ceramics," I thought out loud.

"Then," Kirsten continued, "when the wax melts out of the plaster you fill the resulting hole with melted lead . . . "

"*Melted lead!*" I yelled. "Where in the devil are we supposed to get melted lead?"

She began to look tearful so I quit sorting clothes and hugged her. "Daddy will think of something," I promised.

Marguerite didn't answer her phone so we couldn't borrow any clay. We used crack-fill and it did not set firmly enough to hold the wax until late Sunday night.

On a dusty shelf in the garage my husband unearthed some Babbitt. Grandpa had used it to re-Babbitt the bearings on the NEW IDEAL GIANT horse-drawn mower forty years ago. We bent a lip into a tomato can and Ralph attached vice-grips for a handle. Then, while I held the vice-grips, he applied heat with a blowtorch. We poured the melted lead into the crack-fill mould at about 11:30 Sunday night.

I have thrown away the sticky tray and the ugly pots and the scratchy candle holders, but I think I will keep this little Babbitt bird dropping. I just know it represents something, although I'm not quite sure what.

BEAUTY QUESTIONS WOMEN ASK MOST

THIS HOUSE COLLECTS magazines the way corduroy pants collect lint. From time to time I gather up a pile of them and dump them on the kitchen table. Then I page through them quickly and snip out a few recipes, craft ideas and articles before throwing them away. As I get older, fewer and fewer items attract my attention. I've got thousands of recipes and more craft ideas than I will ever use, and the articles are pretty repetitive. Every magazine features a sure-fire, never-fail diet and a selection of recipes for super-rich desserts. There are a couple of decorating stories, mostly on redoing your kitchen and, lately, a spate of ways to save money.

The health care articles I scan but don't study. I'm past teething and toilet training and not ready for facelifts and geriatrics. There is loads of information on arthritis, migraine, depression, heart disease and cancer. I try not to read these—I'm always afraid I will find a symptom I can identify with.

The last time I did the magazine purge, I didn't find much to save and my job was going quickly, so when I came to "33 Beauty Questions Women Ask Most," I felt I had time to glance through it.

The first ten questions dealt with hair care. Such vital matters as: "What kinds of shampoo should I use? How important is rinsing? How can split ends be prevented? How do I keep my hair from going limp and droopy?"

Nine questions dealt with skin care: "Is soap bad for face cleansing? What can be done about brown spots? Should everyone wear a moisturizer?"

Seven more queries had to do with makeup. "How can I contour my face to give the look of more chiseled cheekbones? How can I prevent eye shadow from creasing? How can I keep my blusher from fading?"

The last seven questions centred on diet and exercise. "Are crash diets really harmful? How many pounds should you lose per week? Do you have to exercise every day?"

This was not an article I felt compelled to keep. Instead I decided to make a quick list of my own—the most frequently asked beauty questions in a house containing children. We will start with when the kids are small: "Who turned up my lipstick without removing the top? Why does the dog smell of cologne? Who dumped the talcum powder on the rug? How can I remove a sliver from your foot when you are screaming and kicking? Where are the Band-aids?"

As the kids grow larger the questions change slightly: "Who left model glue on my good tweezers? Where are the nail clippers? When did you last push back your cuticles? Will you please cut your toenails? Who used the last of the TT and didn't put on a new roll?"

As the kids become teenagers your questions grow more shrill, and occasionally they border on hysteria: "How could you possibly have used that huge bottle of shampoo in one week? For the twelfth time today, will you go shave? Am I the only person in this house who knows how to wash brushes and combs? Who used the last of the TT and didn't put on a new roll?"

Aside from daily bathing, deodorant and occasional lipstick, I don't have much of a beauty routine. The questions I ask myself on this subject are pretty basic: "Will I need a haircut this week? Do I have to wear a skirt and stockings to this affair? How do I get the garden dirt out of my fingernails?"

In a way, that's kind of pitiful. Surely my husband deserves better. Maybe I should go back to the article and find out how to get
"the look of more chiselled cheekbones." And that raises the final
question: how do I find my cheekbones?

INTER-AUTO COMMUNICATION

THERE IS SOMETHING about hurtling along the highway at a death-
defying speed that makes the person hurtling along beside you an
object of great interest. Maybe it's because one gets bored with driving alone and a new face is welcome. Maybe it's because you want to
check and make sure that this fellow traveller looks stable and sober
and unlikely to swerve into your lane. Maybe it's because I'm a farm
person and therefore interested and concerned about even imper-
manent and fleeting neighbours. Whatever the reason, I often find
myself unabashedly studying passengers in passing cars and trying
to guess their characters and destinations by the looks on their faces
and the contents of their vehicles.

A nicely dressed family with a rear window full of gifts wrapped
in white and silver are probably on their way to a wedding. Two or
three older couples, all in suits and good dresses, husbands in front,
wives in the back, could be a funeral or maybe a presbytery meeting.
A serene older couple with a back seat full of toys means a new
grandchild. Young couple, girl clutching a bundle and bouncing like
a coffee perc, back seat full of padded plastic furniture, means first
big trip with the new baby. A big old rusted Chevy with a mis-
matched fender is amusing when driven by a seventeen-year-old,
tragic when it's herded down the highway by an unshaven sixty-five-
year-old in a shabby windbreaker and a greasy baseball cap. There is

the drama of an RCMP van, windows covered with a metal grille and one or two shadowy figures inside, the comedy of little kids who make faces or bare their anatomy from a rear window, and the tragedy when a frazzled mom with a cigarette in her mouth takes one hand from the wheel to smack randomly at as many kids as she can reach.

I enjoy these little forays into the lives of strangers, and mostly I'm content to make my speculations and move on. There are occasions, though, when I want to communicate more fully and toward that end I propose that someone develop an inter-auto communication kit. It could be as simple as big numbers in bright colours and an accompanying code book, so that if someone flashed you a red 3 you could look in your code book and find: "The belt from your trenchcoat is hanging out and dragging in the slush and salt." A large blue 3 might mean: "Your brake lights are not working," and a yellow 3 with a red 2: "You have been signalling a left turn for the last ten miles and I am sick of it and you."

There are other simple, straightforward signals that one number could cover: Your trunk is open, There is liquid (water, I hope) oozing out of the back of your motor home, You have a flat tire on your trailer, Your boat went west at the overpass, I saw you throw that garbage out the window you miserable slob.

Many other situations could not be covered in the code book so easily. Our neighbour George McLeavey had a large, old collie that used to sleep on the top of his truck cab. George didn't always think to look for the dog up there and on several occasions his first clue that the dog was with him was when he braked for a stop sign and old Rover came scrabbling down the windshield and onto the hood. I don't suppose there would be much call for a signal that meant, "There is a large dog spreadeagled on your cab and hanging on by his toenails."

I would like a code sign for "Good grief, lady, how did you get a driver's licence when you are obviously at least 112 years old," and I'd also like one for "Where do you get your hair cut?" I'm not sure how they would send a reply to that last one.

There could even be jokes in the code book, and by flashing *4B* in green you'd have the pleasure of seeing a smile on the face of that harried mother. Well, maybe the first two or three times. Better forget the jokes.

I really think this scheme has possibilities. Maybe I should make a few calls.

KITCHEN *A*RCHAEOLOGY

I WAS TRIMMING a broken fingernail when the clippers slipped from my grasp, hit the linoleum and broke sharply to the left. They disappeared under the stove. My husband came into the kitchen to find me lying on the floor peering into the dusty darkness.

"Having a little rest?" he asked kindly.

"No," I told him, "I am doing some archaeological research. Hand me the yardstick."

"It's a metre stick," he corrected me, "and I think real archaeologists use shovels."

"This is the age of specialization," I said. "My field is kitchen archaeology and of course I need special tools. Many people believe that yardsticks were designed to measure things, but my fellow scientists and I know that they were designed for fishing things out from under refrigerators and stoves."

I made a sweeping motion with the yardstick and a tangle of dust and dog hairs rolled into view. The nail clippers were in the thick of the mess and I gingerly picked them up and blew the dust off them. I poked the remaining mass and examined it as an archaeologist would study a handful of soil at a dig.

The inhabitants of this cave obviously kept domestic animals because canine hair is apparent. The family pet was a short-haired breed, reddish blond in colour and in excellent health according to the texture and shine of the individual hairs.

This was an agricultural community—several seeds and grains were present, including a rather advanced type of barley that would probably germinate if planted. Two examples of the nutritionally insignificant grain popcorn came to light; several of the kernels were in the raw or unexpanded state and two large, puffy morsels had been exposed to controlled heat. As this variety of corn was not grown in northern climates, we must assume that the people of this village carried on some type of trade with a more southern tribe. Because no major waterway services this area, the trade routes remain a mystery.

A shard of pastry-like foodstuff was separated from the dirt mass. Its shape suggested that the original item had been flat, circular and about two inches in diameter. An analysis of the item found large parts of animal fat, refined sugar and ground wheat. As this primitive comestible must have been baked, we can assume that this tribe had the gift of fire and probably toasted their "cookies" on flat hot rocks. The women of the tribe probably wore quantities of jewellery, as evidenced by a number of glass-like beads. No clothing fibres came to light but we must assume rather sophisticated clothing, as a small white button was among the artifacts.

It is thought that these people followed some pagan rite involving nut shells, spruce needles and hard candies. The real significance of this celebration has been lost to us.

A tangle of heavy cord defied analysis, not because I couldn't think of a use but because I could imagine too many. Did they tie their domestic animals? Stitch together animal skins for clothing? Bind tent poles? Hang draperies? Snare small game?

I was pleased with my reasoning and anxious to share my new-found gift for archaeological research with my husband. He listened patiently enough, but I could see that he had something to add.

"There is one more rather obvious conclusion," he said. "The women of this tribe did not spend a whole lot of time cleaning house."

I HATE 𝒮PIDERS

IN THE PALE pre-dawn morning, I had become instantly and completely awake. The bedroom window was a silvery rectangle and the filmy curtains were only muted shadows. There was no sound in the house and no reason why I should be alarmed and wakeful. I turned toward my sleeping husband and was reassured by his peaceful presence. Nothing was upsetting him. I must have dreamed something dangerous. I composed myself to sleep but as I closed my eyes I glimpsed the tiniest wisp of movement.

My knees and elbows flexed for immediate flight, an icy chill ran down my back and I fought the urge to scream. Slowly and stealthily I reached for my glasses, some instinct for preservation demanding that I be able to identify the nameless monster that had invaded our bedroom. With glasses in place I searched the shadows and there it was—a dark, hairy, ugly mass just above the window. It moved again. I gasped and ceased breathing. It took another step, pushed itself from the wall and fell into the shadowy curtains. My body jerked convulsively and I stifled a scream.

Ralph turned toward me, opened his eyes and groaned. "It's a spider, isn't it? You're wearing your glasses so it must be a big one. If it was a small one you'd have the binoculars."

I pointed wordlessly at the curtains. He—sweet, patient man— found a tissue, caught the spider and returned to sleep. I lay there wide awake till morning. Do spiders travel in pairs? Where was its mate? Maybe it came with a family. I kept my glasses on.

I hate spiders. They are so ugly, so malevolent, they carry an aura of horror and mystery with them. They move so quickly and so silently, they inhabit the night and they came from mouldy, oozy, slimy places and have witnessed horrible crimes and nameless dreads. They eat flies. I hate them.

Everyone in my family has tried to reason with me. Spiders are interesting and unique, they tell me. They are not insects, they are arachnids. They have delicate bodies and are more terrified of you than you are of them. They eat harmful insects and are beneficial to mankind. Their webs are beautiful and a miracle of engineering. I still hate spiders.

"Read *Charlotte's Web*," my kids said. "It will give you a whole new insight into spiders. Charlotte is downright lovable." Well, I read it and Charlotte *is* wonderful, but the horrible, creepy uglies that I find in the cellar aren't Charlotte.

One day when Carl Pearson's mother, Mrs. George Pearson, lived above Beckners' food store, she reached out to brush a dead leaf from a windowsill. The dead leaf jumped away. It was a tarantula, and the only explanation is that it had come to Carstairs in a big stalk of bananas.

Ever since I heard that story I have approached bananas with extreme caution. If I had been in Mrs. Pearson's place, they would have found me dead, my hair turned snow white and my face frozen in a grimace of terror.

We took a poll of fears at a Women's Institute meeting once. Our fears, in this order, were: bats, mice, snakes, wasps, spiders, moths, needles, bulls.

I'd try to defend my loved ones from most of the above and I'd even make a fair stand against a cougar or a grizzly. But not against spiders. I really hate spiders.

THE LAWN *O*RNAMENT VENDETTA

IN AUGUST 1984 I wrote a column on plastic lawn ornaments and my aversion to them. Flamingos left out in snow bother me especially, but I also touched on gnomes, donkeys, lambs with dirt where their lungs should be and various non-indigenous species parked lifelessly in otherwise attractive flower beds.

I have had a lot of fun with that column. People phoned to tell me about dreadful statuary they had seen and stopped me on the street to agree with my stand on flamingos, and as recently as last month someone asked for a copy to send to a friend in another province.

The lawn ornament story did not end with the written word. In the early morning after Halloween 1985, I peered groggily into our yard and screamed. Crouched on the lawn in nesting position was a gleaming white pelican. For one wild moment I considered phoning the Audubon Society, but the pelican's unnatural stillness and the note taped to his black beak were reasonable indications that this was not your average waterfowl.

The great pelican mystery was finally solved when friends invited us to dinner and confessed. Peli the pelican became a receptacle for old Christmas cards, and on the following Halloween I nearly broke my neck poking around in the dark to plant a solitary flamingo in the yard of those who had donated Peli.

Some time later, on a sparkling morning early one summer, I was making my usual tour through the yard when a flash of fluorescent pink halted me in mid-step. There in the lupins lurked a dreaded pink flamingo. I couldn't have been more surprised if it had been a hippopotamus. How could a flamingo have arrived here in our backyard without my knowing it? And what of our sharp-toothed, overprotective dog? Shaking my head in disbelief I started for the house, only to be stopped in mid-step once again. For there, peering around a peony, was flamingo number two.

It took a long time and a lot of phone calls to find the flamingo furnishers. Finally I was sure I knew their identity, and I began to plan my revenge.

In August, when several of us were gathered for my dad's birthday, Mom drew my attention to one of his gifts. This was a present that gives real meaning to the saying: "It's the thought that counts." A pale green moss-like growth oozed up and over the sides of a hollow-bodied ceramic swordfish. As the unfortunate fish had lost part of his tail and the fungus-like matter resembled fur rather than fins, the overall effect was of a slow-witted green hedgehog. I had found just the gift for my flamingo-fancying friends.

Late that night my little niece Kate and I embarked on our errand. I had drawn Kate a map of our friends' yard, driveway and patio, and the picnic table where the plant should be placed. Kate studied the map with the intensity of a freedom fighter. On the way over we passed several large seismic vehicles parked for the night. Kate jumped involuntarily. She had so entered into the spirit of our adventure that she imagined them to be military vehicles guarding some top-secret installation. I calmed her as best I could, but by now her palms were so damp that she could hardly hold the hedgehog.

I parked the truck just beyond our friends' windbreak and turned off the lights. Their windows were still lit, so Kate knew that she was in danger of detection, but this only added to her excitement. She stepped out onto the road clutching the plant and I watched her tiptoe into the driveway. In a remarkably short time I caught glimpses of her pale sweater flitting past trees on the return trip. She was running flat out and I could imagine her tripping over something in the dark and being gravel-skinned from nose to navel. She made it to the truck safely and leapt inside.

"Thank you, Auntie," she gasped, "for giving me this opportunity to become a criminal."

Wonderful, I thought—I have launched a ten-year-old girl into a life of crime. But at least the lawn ornament vendetta was over.

TECHNOLOGICALLY IMPAIRED

MY GOOD OLD MIXER is about to go to the old appliance garage in the sky. The tips are gone from its beaters, the markings are worn off the dial, the handle had to be reattached with the glue gun. It changes speed by itself now, gearing down when it's stressed. It heats up until I can hardly touch it and what it has lost in power it has gained in noise.

I'd like to buy a new mixer. I'd like to buy one exactly like the one I'm retiring, but my kids think this is silly and backward of me. "Get the Sunbeam Kitchen Centre," they say. "Electronic mixer, blender, slicer, shredder, salad maker, food processor and dough maker. All in one unit."

I looked up the Kitchen Centre in my catalogues and everything the kids say is true. It also has electronic touch control, sixteen speeds, digital readout, three cutting discs, stainless steel blades and a storage lid. The storage lid part I can understand, but what do I want with "electronic touch control," for heaven's sake? And what in the world is the "digital readout"? Do little squared-off letters appear, saying "You forgot the eggs, stupid," or "Did you turn on the oven?" or maybe just "Have a nice day."

I am a reasonably strong and healthy person, coordinated enough to tie my own shoes and knit (although not simultaneously) and bright enough to follow a complex recipe or sewing pattern. Why can't I program the VCR? Why don't I use the microwave beyond defrost and high? Seven of its nine settings have never been tested. I can't even remember how to reset its miserable clock.

Our eldest son, through threats and bribery, forced me to learn how to use the computer—at least the word processor and printer. Now I don't know how I ever managed without them, and if I had to go back to an ordinary typewriter I'd feel terribly deprived. But even as I take pleasure in what I can do, I have this nasty nagging feeling that I am using the computer to about one zillionth of its potential and if I had my wits about me I'd have computerized all the farm records, recipes and Christmas card lists and be able, with the touch of a key, to tell you how many milligrams of pyrethrin/piperonyl butoxide one needs to eliminate thrips and leaf hoppers from mangelwurzels. Supposing anyone cared to know.

I used the cruise control on the car once. It was by accident and I nearly gave myself a heart attack. I have a solar-powered calculator in my purse. I don't know why, as on the rare occasions that I use it, I don't trust it and recheck all the numbers by hand. I have never used a fax machine. I hate answering machines and once when I called my future daughter-in-law and got an answering tape, I got so confused over what my relationship was to her that I gave the machine my maiden name.

I hate childproof lids on medicine bottles, and any kid can open one faster than any grandma. I loathe the tamper-proof lid on a certain jug of cooking oil and I nearly went mad trying to screw on the lid of the gas tank in our little truck.

When we bought the new stereo, the kids said it was only reasonable to get one that played CDs, even though we had none at the time—we had tapes and LPs. The tapes were not a problem, but what would become of our records? Our son wired the old turntable into the new unit and it seems to work, but I have no idea how or why.

A few years ago a Japanese company modernized the toilet through microelectronics. It is now possible to have a one-stop checkup simply by using the toilet in your own bathroom. Sensors will detect and measure levels of sugar, protein, red and white blood cells and ketones, and the results will be displayed on a screen. You may also detect pulse, blood pressure and temperature by sticking your finger into a gadget in the toilet's armrest.

Not in this house, not in my lifetime and certainly not until I have learned to program the VCR.

REBEL WITHOUT A COSTUME

OUR KIDS STARTED trick-or-treating when Mark was two and two-thirds years old and John ten and a half months. The kids hadn't exactly begged to go. Mark didn't really know what Halloween was and John wasn't talking much, so the truth is they went for my pleasure. I hadn't thought of taking them until the last minute so their costumes suffered from spontaneity, but we took them to the homes of three or four dear friends and the cherubic shepherd and tottery devil (no one walks well at ten and a half months) were received with delight.

The next year I started planning earlier. Mark was a knight in armour. He wore a shirt of chain mail, plumed bleach bottle helmet and tights made from the good parts of two old Teflon ironing board covers. John, his faithful squire, wore a green jerkin over red sweater and tights. His belt was a rope and he carried Mark's extra sword. A year later, when Kirsten was eleven months old, they were all green caterpillars with big black velvet spots, silver eyes and antennae.

On succeeding Halloweens we had robots, ghosts, mummies, chickens, hillbillies, hoboes and monsters. I loved Halloween and fortunately the kids were good sports about it. Up to a point that is.

As Kirsten's grade two Halloween party approached, I suggested possible costumes and finally she agreed to be a ghost. We assembled a sheet, a derby hat, neck chain and blue rubber gloves, and on the day of the party I handed her a bag containing these items.

"I don't want a costume," she said.

"Honey," I told her, "this is the day of the party. Everyone will have a costume."

"I don't want a costume."

"Look, Kirsten," I said, "you agreed on the ghost, but I guess I could find John's old mummy costume, or the robot thing."

"I don't want a costume."

Two minutes to bus time was never my most rational period so I let her go. But as lunchtime—party time—approached, I became more and more concerned. Finally I snatched up the bag, jumped in the car and drove to Cremona. I had Kirsten sent out into the hall and we conferred.

"Sweetheart," I whispered, "I was afraid you'd be wishing you had a costume so I brought the—"

She interrupted me. "I don't want a costume."

"Why don't you want a costume?"

"I just don't want one."

"Look, kid, for my sake wear this costume. Do you want to be the only child here in civvies? People will think you have a rotten mother."

"I'm not the only one. Cora-Sue is in plain clothes."

"Cora-Sue," I snarled. "Isn't she the little girl who couldn't finish her popsicle-stick bread basket because her mother fell asleep on the table? Put on the lousy costume."

I had inadvertently raised my voice during this exchange and I am afraid I had also gripped my daughter's shoulder with something more than motherly affection. She began to look tearful. She shrank away from my hand and glanced apprehensively toward her classroom door. A new teacher whom I did not recognize walked past us. She raised her eyebrows knowingly. Now I was not only a rotten mother who couldn't be bothered to costume her child, I was also suspected of child abuse.

It was time to give up. There is no logic in forcing a child to have fun. I patted Kirsten's head and turned away in defeat, just as Joyce Pawson came down the hall carrying a plate of fudge for the party.

"And what is Wade dressed as?" I asked. I was hoping that she would say, "Nothing, he didn't want a costume," but no such luck. He was a leopard, complete with whiskers and tail.

"This is such an exciting time for the kids," Joyce said. "They get such a kick out of the party and their costumes! But you know, there are always one or two poor little guys with no costumes at all. It's such a shame—some mothers just don't seem to care."

HALLOWEEN *M*AGIC

I CAME HOME one evening in late October just at that magic time
when the waning light has drained all colour from the landscape but
left behind sharp blacks and pale, gleaming greys. Because there are
no shadows and no reflections, this is the time to really see the bone
structure of a tree. It's also a lovely time to see owls, and when I saw
an unmistakable owl shape against the sky, I slowed the car.

He was perched at the top of a tree, his horns showing clear and
clean against the sky. His head and breast loomed large in relation to
his rump and tail, but when he spread his wings he became
magnificent and powerful, and perfectly proportioned. He was a real
Halloween owl and suddenly my heart filled with all the things that
meant Halloween when I was a kid.

The Halloween nights of my memory were all crisp and clean
and moonlit. The roads that were so friendly and familiar in daylight
became shrouded trails that led to danger. Our school ponies caught
our excitement and became prancing, skittish creatures ready to
burst into headlong flight at our frequent self-induced terrors. We
rode out into the countryside, bent on mischief.

Pretty mild mischief—opening chicken house doors, tripping
the switch on a power pole, putting junk in mailboxes, tying door-
knobs to porch railings. The primary purpose of the exercise was to
scare ourselves into a delightful state of nutsiness.

We began the evening by riding from farm to farm collecting our
"gang." At every house a mother, father or both came out to be assured that yes, we were warm enough, and no, we wouldn't do anything dangerous or stupid. Even as these promises left our mouths
we hoped that something dangerous, stupid and unavoidable would
present itself.

With the group assembled, the evening truly began. We moved
off into the darkness alternately whispering, as though approaching
a rustlers' campsite, and shrieking as though pursued by Indians.

At first we talked of other Halloweens. The time Cece Murphy shot his gun into the air and so enraged the neighbourhood. The time live turkeys were loosed in Ericksons' kitchen. The time everyone lay quietly waiting for Evan Holt to shut off his light, and when he finally did and they prepared to attack, Bobby had gone to sleep under a tree and had to be found and awakened.

Next came the terrible stories, how long ago, some young men "borrowed" a piece of machinery from a dealer's lot and pushed it down the main street. The town constable ran into the street calling "Halt!" but the machine's momentum was such that the boys could not stop and they ran over him and killed him. In this same category was the story of Len deBoer. As he walked home one dark Halloween night his brother leapt out from behind a tree, to scare him. Len had been playing ball and was carrying a baseball bat, and he conked his brother on the head, killing him instantly.

Then we got into the really scary stuff. The sales rep for Raleigh Home products had told someone's mother that he once stopped at a house where a maniac was chained to a bedpost. We had no reason to believe that the poor soul was anywhere near us but we convinced ourselves that the grimy little shack of a local bachelor was the logical place for just such an inmate. The fact that no one had ever seen the interior of the house was all the proof we needed.

By this time our imaginations had taken over and all kinds of horrible things were loosed. We saw open graves in the gravel pit, dismembered bodies in ditches. A skull gleamed from a fence post and werewolves waited in culverts. We had now reached saturation point and anything—an unexpected sound, a sudden gust of wind, a startled pony—was the catalyst that sent us screaming home to warmth and safety.

Halloween magic. I bet it's still out there on a moonlit October night when coyotes sing and an owl drifts past the moon.

I'LL BE ℬRINGING
A FEW THINGS HOME

LIKE MOST FAMILIES, ours went through a period when none of our three children was officially "at home" any more, but neither did they officially have homes of their own. We were at that awful in-between stage when adult children need someplace to store the things that they have accumulated. Everywhere cupboards and closets, attics and drawers were stuffed with their possessions. The chest of drawers that I had hoped to use for fabric was full of computer books and disks. The upstairs closet that should have taken Ralph's and my off-season clothes held sleeping bags, a mattress, Lego, Meccano, musical instruments and old textbooks. Kirsten's plates, mugs and crystal crowded the china cabinet. "My" records were squashed into one-eighth of "my" record cabinet. Books were everywhere, two and three deep on the shelves, heaped on the stairs, mounded on the coffee tables. The kids' extra bedding filled the blanket box and their extra boots and shoes filled the entry.

Our son Mark's job as a computer instructor kept him on the road from September to late April one year and he knew he would be in Norway for the month of May, so it seemed silly to pay rent on an apartment he'd rarely use. He moved home in October.

"There's not that much stuff, Mom," he said. "Will my filing cabinet fit in the guest room closet?"

"Only if I throw out my fabric and yarn that got displaced by your computer stuff," I said grimly.

"My Ikea furniture knocks down," he assured me, "and I'll just slide the bed parts and shelves into the west attic."

"Will it fit in around your old toy box, race set and scuba gear?" I asked.

"I guess not," he admitted. "Well, I'll just slip the whole package in behind the Hide-a-Bed in the playroom, and since that will make opening the bed sort of difficult maybe I can put my camera equipment, albums, pictures and a few more books and records right on the sofa, okay?"

I looked around the room. Every flat surface was already covered with computers and computer parts, bits of sound systems, tools, wires, tapes and electronic things that I couldn't identify.

"Go ahead," I told him, "but if I need more bed space be prepared to give up your room."

He's a nice guy, this eldest son. We love him dearly and are happy to have him home. But he is not neat.

"You are just like your father," I told him, "strong-willed and messy. You will either have to learn to pick up after yourself or do what your Dad did and marry a woman who is servile and tidy."

Mark's eyes widened in amazement. "I didn't know Dad had been married before," he said. "What happened to her?"

It's true—I am not neat; neither am I servile. What I am is a pack-rat and a collector. I have enough odd balls of wool to knit mitts for all the street people in Vancouver. Enough fabric scraps to put patchwork quilts on every bed in Cremona. I have sufficient blue jean pieces to patch every day for the rest of my life, craft projects and magazines to keep me busy until I'm 112, books to read until my glasses wear out and enough jelly jars for the County of Mountain View.

Because of this serious character flaw I couldn't, with any authority, lecture the kids on neatness. All I could do was squash things in tighter, add another layer to the pile of books, send another bag to the Salvation Army.

After John, our number two son, had defended his thesis and received his Master's degree, he too decided to go to Norway in May and was not quite sure what he would be doing for the rest of the summer.

"Mom," he said diffidently, "it seems pretty silly to pay rent on my apartment from May to August, so I guess I'll be bringing a few things home."

The UN named 1987 the Year of Shelter for the Homeless. If one more thing comes into this home, Ralph and I may be listed among those in need.

LATE *N*IGHT TALK WITH A CLOCK

MY HUSBAND got one of those neat little clock radios for his birthday. It's an LED, and it's added a whole new dimension to insomnia.

It's one of those nights when you aren't worried, there is no unusual noise in the house, you don't hurt anywhere, don't need to go to the bathroom, don't know why you are lying there wakeful, but you do know that it is 4:31. The bright red, silent, squared-off computer numbers say 4:31, and if you lie there wide awake and watch, they will soundlessly change to 4:32.

Ralph is a large, warm, peaceful heap and I have no desire to disturb him, so it's just me and the clock keeping watch in the night. We stare at each other and the clock says 4:33. Clock and I have devised a couple of quiet games to while away our vigil, and I'm willing to share these games in case you or any other reader ends up in similar circumstances.

One of them is Do It Yourself Eye Test. Close one eye and observe Clock for a count of ten. Change eyes and count ten again. Could you see Clock with either eye? This proves that both of your eyeballs are still functioning.

A note of warning here: if one eye seems to have stopped working, remain calm. Do not leap up screaming. Simply rise quietly on one elbow and try again—your husband's shoulder or a bit of bedding has probably obstructed your line of view.

When you change eyes, does the LED display leap alarmingly from left to right or right to left? This may or may not prove that you have astigmatism. I don't know in which eye, or how bad, but it is nothing to panic over. Why do you suppose you wear glasses?

When you tire of playing Eye Test, try Test Your Timing. In this game, you try to count to sixty in the exact length of time it takes Clock to change from 4:41 to 4:42. The instant Clock says 4:41, begin counting silently. If you are a good judge of the breadth of a second, you will be reaching sixty just as Clock changes to 4:42.

This game used to be transferable to one's family car. Driving at exactly 60 mph, you could try to count to sixty in exactly the time it took your odometer to register one mile. But I've given up this game because now we drive at 100 km/h and I haven't figured out whether you're supposed to count to a hundred or sixty or something in between. Besides, it makes conversation difficult—34 Sit down and be quiet, 35 I don't have any gum, 36 Get your feet off the seat, 37 Shut that window, 38 Look! a deer!, 39 I've missed the bloody corner.

Clock now says 4:59. Maybe I should just get up and quietly patch some coveralls, or I could have the kitchen floor all washed and dry before anyone else wakes up. Is it light enough to go out and sweep the deck? It's probably cold outside, and it's so warm here and peaceful and quiet and good night, Clock.

MAYBE I'LL *V*ACUUM TOMORROW

OUR HOUSE IS FILLED with handmade things that have varying degrees of value and varying degrees of artistic merit. I know that some people think that handicrafts give your house that "cottage" look, but I don't care what some people think. It's my house and my taste, my choice and mostly my handicraft. There are quilted cushions, cross-stitch samplers and pictures, crewel work, needlepoint, Norweave wall hangings, Hardanger runners on the buffet and cedar chest, pictures that I have framed, furniture and shelves that I have sanded, stained and varnished. I have made my own curtains, shams, duvet covers and bedskirts. I have knit a zillion sweaters, crocheted afghans, embroidered tablecloths, polished rocks and even beaded mukluks. I have sewn a million outfits in every size from doll up, made multi Raggedy Anns and all the characters from *Winnie the Pooh.* I have smocked baby dresses and mended two thousand pairs of jeans and twice that many socks. And why, may you ask, have I been such a compulsive Suzy Homemaker? Is it because I am so very creative and artistic? Well, no. I mostly do it to avoid vacuuming.

I will do anything to put off running the vacuum cleaner. I hate the vacuum cleaner and all that it stands for. Actually, my vacuum cleaner doesn't stand very well, and that is one of the reasons I hate it. Leave the miserable thing unattended while you pick up an errant book and it leans over and whacks a piece out of a table leg. It's a Centra-Vac, which means that "there is no heavy canister to carry from room to room." Yeah, well, thirty feet of dead python is not exactly light either, especially when the python coils itself around a chair leg and jerks you up short, arranges itself into a pile that you back into and trip over, or uses its ribs to grate the edges off of door frames and corners.

For about ten years I didn't vacuum, ever. I paid the kids to do it. To encourage them to get into all the corners, I offered a bonus of five cents for every fly and ten cents for every spider, alive or dead. My husband has vacuumed for me on occasion. He is not much on corners and he can't be bribed, but there will be no complaints from me. Once in a while one of my sisters will take pity and once in a while I have a cleaning lady, but often—too often—I have to do it myself. I can feel hair sticking to the back of my neck and sweat running into my eyes. And that's while I'm getting the rotten thing out of the broom closet.

My current vacuum cleaner does not pick up cat hair, just sort of redistributes it. But otherwise it is fairly efficient, and because the motor is in the basement, it is not terribly noisy. That is the good news. The bad news is that like all vacuum cleaners, it does not get close enough to the baseboards, it doesn't go tight into corners and it will eat whatever it can catch—the jumble of wires that connect VCR, TV and stereo, the ball of yarn that the cat rolled under the couch. And you don't soon forget the sound of a power head eating a twelve-foot phone cord or tearing the fringe off of a throw rug.

Little bedside tables laden with hand lotion, Kleenex, a phone, four books, a notebook, some pencils and maybe a magazine or two are inclined to dump their loads if you look at them. Come by with a vacuum cleaner and they throw themselves halfway across the bedroom floor. Big, heavy tables force you to decide whether to move them and make new rug dents or go with the old until they are permanent. Do you take off the head and do all the corners at once, or switch back and forth as you change rooms? Is this the day to move the couch, and do you dare reach blindly under the stove without checking first to see what's under there? I hate to vacuum.

Today is almost gone, what with doing the other chores and writing this down, so of course I can't be expected to vacuum today. But tomorrow, maybe. Although it has been ages since I wrote to Aunt Georgia, the geraniums in the basement really need attention, the amaryllis should be repotted and there are those bread covers I want to cross-stitch for gifts. Maybe Saturday morning. Maybe Monday. Maybe never!

"BUT YOU'RE *So* ISOLATED"

WHEN WE DECIDED to take over the family farm, one of my Calgary friends shook her head doubtfully and said, "I just can't imagine you as a farm woman. What will you do all day?"

I wasn't sure what I'd do all day either. I supposed I'd have lots of time to take lovely walks with my children, enjoy the changing seasons, catch up on my reading and sewing. I had lived on a farm as a child so I knew something of gardens and animals and I looked forward to the serenity and peace after the hustle and bustle of the city.

I became, of course, busier than I had ever been in my life, and as I adjusted to the frantic rural pace I became less and less tolerant of my city friends' misconceptions.

One of Ralph's former co-workers arrived while I was up to my elbows in green peas. "Hey," he said in surprise, "you've got running water and electricity."

"I know there's a lot of work on a farm," said another friend, "but what do you do for fun?"

I have an answer for that but good taste prevents my giving it.

In the same vein a Calgary couple invited us to a concert at the Jubilee Auditorium. I was somewhat bewildered when the lady began telling me what type of clothing people generally wore to these functions. Obviously she thought that as a simple country woman I had never been to the Jubilee. Shades of the Beverly Hillbillies—did she think we'd show up in overalls and rubber boots? Or maybe we'd rent tux and tiara?

"I was at a farm home once and it was almost like a city home." This from one of my former co-workers.

It's hard to argue with a statement this vague, but I know some farm homes that would compare with the city's finest and I have seen some Calgary homes that no farmer would use as a chicken coop.

"But you're so isolated."

Lady, this is called privacy. I don't suppose you have ever before seen uncorrupted privacy. Drop in sometime on a summer weekend. The kids call it Disneyland North.

"Your children will have so few of the advantages, and don't you worry about the quality of education in a country school?"

Our children's piano lessons included juice, cookies, love, Christmas and birthday presents, and a friendship that continues to this day. They learned to swim first through the Cremona Swim Project and then from a dear friend with a private pool in this neighbourhood. They all had years with the County Band, belonged to Explorers and Cubs, and had ready access to Sunday School, 4-H, softball, hockey, basketball, tennis, curling, golf, ballet, gymnastics, etc., etc.

All of our kids did well at science fairs and the education they got at Cremona led them into university degrees. They had, and still have, horses, dogs, cats, rabbits, chickens and pet calves. They have had unlimited clean space to play in, with creeks, trees and flowers. They have learned to work. They have seen birth and death. I don't know what advantages they missed. Skateboarding maybe.

Last April a Winnipeg newspaper did a survey in a shopping centre and a public library entitled "Farm Women through the eyes of their City Sisters."

Here are some of the perceptions our city sisters shared:

"On a farm TV is their whole life, what else is there to do?"

"I went into a milking barn and was amazed at how clean it was. No getting up at 6:00 AM to milk cows any more, they just turn on the milking machines."

"They are overweight because they make pies a lot."

"Farm wives have more work, fewer worries, bigger breasts and look a lot frumpier than their urban counterparts."

Closer to home a recent *Alberta Report* says that "Alberta Women's Institute caters to needy rural women." This infuriates me. There are 2,200 AWI members in Alberta and they are a pretty good cross-section of farm women. I am proud to be one of them. I would like to give *Alberta Report* the benefit of the doubt and suggest that they meant "the needs of rural women."

Meanwhile, if anyone shows up on my isolated doorstep with a food hamper, they had better be prepared to wear it.

A TIME TO REAP

I AM ESPECIALLY PRONE to nostalgia in the fall. For one thing, it is the end of the growing season. The grain is ripe and ready for harvest, the garden is almost finished, the flowers that haven't gone to seed will soon freeze. At this point in all these life cycles one can't help but contemplate one's own mortality.

For another thing, I've been canning. Putting aside food to feed your family during the winter is surely one of the most basic female nurturing instincts, and it is an exercise that brings me closer to my roots. These roots aren't that remote—I make crabapple jelly from Ralph's mom's recipe, using apples from her tree and straining the juice through her colander. Mom never used a jelling agent and she showed me how to test the jelly's readiness by dipping a fork in it. If the space between the tines fills and remains filled with a somewhat firm and elastic membrane, the jelly is ready. As I peer at my fork and try to make the call, I can almost hear Mom's voice: "Don't make the mistake I did when I started to make jelly. I boiled it so long that I wouldn't have needed to put lids on the jars—the mice couldn't bite through it."

I often feel close to Mom Olson, this place was so much a part of her. I carry my glowing jars of jelly downstairs and arrange them on the shelves that Dad made. I wonder if the next generation will do this.

I can fruit by the open-kettle method, the way my mother taught me. I use the jars she gave me and the same type of syrup. I use her beet pickle recipe too. I know that the open-kettle method is fraught with peril, and that I should use a canner and process the jars in a hot-water bath. I know all these things but my mom never poisoned anybody, nor did Grandma, nor will I, and if I am going to do this Harrowsmith-roots thing I am going to do it authentically.

Some years ago, when my mom was only about eighty, she watched me ladle jelly into jars and said, "Can't you just pour that from the kettle?"

"No," I said, "I can't. I'll spill all over the place."

"It's easier to just pour from the kettle," she repeated.

"Mom," I said, "I've tried that. It sheets and slops and messes up the outside of the jars."

"Would you just let me try it?" she asked.

So I moved out of her way and she hoisted the heavy, hot Dutch oven and filled all the jars without spilling a drop.

Mom didn't have a freezer when we were growing up, but she had an enormous garden and she canned gallons of vegetables. She used a canner, and I can remember waking in the night to hear her stoking the stove because the jars of peas had to boil for something like seven hours. Mom's canned corn was such a special treat that one quart was always saved for Christmas dinner. We ate so much cabbage relish and beet pickles that they doubled as vegetables, and her dill pickles were better than Bick's.

I remember the year of the enormous saskatoon crop, when we canned two hundred quarts of them. I was working at the Treasury Branch but didn't start until 8:30 AM, so Dad would call us at 5:30 AM and we would go out in the country and pick until 8:00. After the fourth or fifth day he quit calling me. The way he tells it, I'd get two inches of fruit in my pail then see a spider, scream and throw my berries in the air.

And that's why autumn sends me into introspection and nostalgia. It's a time to reaffirm family traditions, a time to remember our roots. Not the time to sow, but the time to reap.

WINTER

Ralph keeps the feeders full, I hang the suet, and in return chickadees, nuthatches, downy woodpeckers and hairy woodpeckers, red polls, pine siskins, waxwings and grosbeaks bring us life and energy and make the winter bearable.

Our winter landscape is truly beautiful. When the garden and the fields beyond are covered in fresh snow, spruce trees are almost black against a clear blue sky and a family of dainty deer eat fallen apples under big trees coated in hoar-frost. It's sometimes hard to breathe. Winter sunrises are so filled with red, purple, cerise and mauve that we have to guard against taking yet another picture. Dark, clear winter nights are wonderful for star watching. Winter cows in their thick, furry coats look like live teddy bears and are almost cuddly. I love snow crunching underfoot, little snowsuited kids on sleds, a fire in the wood stove. But I am not a winter person.

When our son John was little, he looked out on a bitterly cold morning and said, "If it weren't for Christmas they could just skip winter altogether." I'm with you, John. I love Christmas, but I hate icy roads and cold cars and bulky gloves and boots. My coats always seem too heavy and not warm enough. Ice is only good for putting in tall glasses, and snow is only good for snow cones.

If it weren't for Christmas. I love Christmas carols and Christmas concerts. I love to make my Mom's Christmas pudding and Ralph's mother's cake. I want to do all the traditional cookies and write and receive letters and give and get gifts. I want to gather in all my family and put up the biggest tree we have room for and as soon as it comes down I want to start looking at my seed catalogues. I am not a winter person.

SHOE-CREAM IF *N*ECESSARY

ON A BITTER COLD winter day a frozen package of last summer's raspberries can renew my faith in nature. All I have to do is put the plastic carton in the microwave for about ten minutes of auto-defrost, and the berries are as perfect as they were in August. We can even pretend that they are delicately sun-warmed. One winter day when I opened just such a package, there on top were four perfect berries, still attached to stems and leaves. The mark of Hatsue.

Hatsue Inui was sixteen when she came to stay with us for a few weeks on a student exchange program. Her home is in Yokohama and her limited English improved enormously during her month with us. We enjoyed her very much. She was sweet, funny, helpful, cute and bright. We loved her. Hatsue's talent for picking and arranging artistic raspberry packages was only one of her many facets. Her hobbies included hiking, playing the piano and cooking, and cooking was her favourite.

Hats often confused "if possible" with "if necessary," and one afternoon as she and I drove home from town, she turned to me and said sweetly, "If necessary, I will make shoe-cream."

"Shoe-cream," I repeated uncomprehendingly. "Shoe-cream, shoo-cream, show-crème. I'm sorry Hats, I don't understand."

"Shoe-cream," she repeated patiently, and when she saw that I still didn't understand she furrowed her brow and looked thoughtful. I knew she was trying to think of a new way to approach the problem.

I tried too. Perhaps shoe-cream was a homemade Japanese shoe cleaner. Would it be a general shoe cleaner? Hats, like every other teenager, wore joggers. Would it be a bleach formula for joggers, or was she planning to clean the men's western boots? It wouldn't surprise me—Hats was a very willing and cheerful helper.

"What does shoe-cream look like?" I asked.

Hats thought for a moment, then smiled brightly. "Looks like little cabbages."

Aha, that eliminates shoe polish, and little cabbages must be Brussels sprouts. "Do you mean Brussels sprouts, Hats?"

She looked uncertain.

"I don't have any in the garden," I continued, "but if it is important to you I will buy a package of frozen ones."

"Garden?" said Hatsue doubtfully. "Frozen?"

"How will you prepare the Brussels sprouts?" I asked.

"Very simple preparation," she answered. "Cut off top, hollow out centre and fill with sweet custard cream."

It sounded horrible. I didn't know what to say—I did not want to hurt her feelings.

"Hats honey," I said diplomatically, "I don't think the family would eat it. I don't think custard cream would go well with such a strongly flavoured vegetable."

For an instant she looked crestfallen. Then, "Vegetable?" she squeaked. "Shoe-cream is not vegetable, shoe-cream is very nice dessert."

In a dim recess of my unilingual brain a light clicked on—choux-crème. *Choux* is the French word for cabbage and choux-paste makes cream puffs that look like little cabbages.

"Cream puffs, Hats!" I yelled. "Little French pastries with whipped cream or custard inside."

"Yes, yes!" She clapped her hands delightedly. "Very nice choux-crème. Family *will* eat. I do not put egg cream inside vegetable."

Oh Hats, so many things remind us of you. Origami storks still nest in my cactus. Fans, lanterns and Japanese postcards decorate the guest room. The prettily arranged raspberries bring you close to us and none of us will ever again see cream puffs without thinking of shoe-cream.

Hatsue's parents telephoned us to thank us for caring for their daughter, and Father invited us to stay in his home when we go to Japan. We would like very much to accept his invitation, because for us Japan no longer seems so strange or far away. Almost as if we had family there.

FEAR, BLIND FAITH, PANIC AND ICE

AFTER HIS EYE SURGERY my husband was supposed to have a few weeks of not bending over and not lifting heavy things. This meant that I went with him to do chores, feeding chop to the steers, opening gates, pulling the strings off bales and mostly yelling, "Please let me do that," "That's got to be more than ten pounds," and "Wait for me!"

I love being with Ralph under any circumstances, but I am not a winter person. Oh, I love the colour in winter sunrises and sunsets—purple, turquoise and pink, navy, royal and scarlet. I love the birds on our feeders and I adore Christmas, but that's it. I hate cold, I hate any ice that won't fit in a tall glass, I hate boots and gloves and bulky coats, and warm headgear gives me claustrophobia. I hate having to be careful when I walk. Mostly I hate icy roads.

Our daughter-in-law helped us out by doing some of the driving to eye appointments when the side roads and some tree-shaded areas were downright treacherous.

"I was off the road here once," I said casually, "and here and back there."

She looked at me quizzically and I knew that she was wondering about my driving ability. I am not a great driver but when you consider that I spent most of my mothering years in the car, it is a wonder I wasn't in the ditch more often. Real loneliness is waiting for the band bus at 11:30 PM while snow swirls past your windshield so thickly that you can't see your hood ornament. Fear is one of your passengers when your three little kids are huddled together in the back seat, the entire landscape is uniformly pale grey and moving left to right and you—poor, fallible mortal mommy—are not sure where the road ends and the ditch begins. Blind faith is going on up the hill when the feathery little spruces just two feet from your right front fender are probably the tops of forty-foot trees. Panic is when you drive over the top of a hill and see glare ice and cars at odd angles all the way down.

At around the same time, *Reader's Digest* ran an article on winter driving, and their advice on skid recovery is to "stay off the brakes and steer where you want the car to go." Oh whoop de do, show me a person who is skidding sideways past fence posts at 80 km/h and doesn't hit the brakes and I'll show you a person with very poor reflexes. If you are fast enough to catch a baby after he leaps from his high chair and before he hits the floor you are going to hit the brakes without time for conscious thought. As for "steering where you want the car to go," that's a little redundant, isn't it? That's what I had been doing when the whole mess began and look where it got me.

One night when I had a meeting in town, driving in was nasty because my headlights were dirty from the salt sand on the highway and a creeping fog cut my vision even more. On the way home the fog lifted and I could see a bit better, but spots that had been icy on the way in were now, because of the damp fog, absolutely glassy. I began to creep home, aiming for bare patches and praying.

Without any warning my car cut sharply left. I have no idea in which direction I steered and there was no question of "stay off the brakes." The car cut right, changed ends and whipped into the ditch backwards. Fence posts flew past my window in reverse order. The car stalled and stopped, the snow settled. It was very quiet down there. As ditches go this was not a terribly deep one. Nothing ventured, nothing gained, I thought. I started the car, drove out of the ditch and went home.

I didn't show anyone the spot where I went off the road. I think if you can drive out by yourself, it shouldn't go on your record.

MY *L*AST CATALOGUE

SEVERAL YEARS AGO the *TV Guide* carried an ad for a "cordless light fixture." The ad read, "Requires no wiring. Light up those dark closets and gloomy stairwells. Batteries not included." Well, I just happened to have a dark closet that regularly drove me to near violence. Just try to sort black velour from brown velvet when you're standing between it and the feeble light from a bedside lamp, while using one hand and one knee to keep four blankets and a quilt from sliding into an open trunk. My main worry is that I will grab something that grabs back. I have a horror of spiders and sometimes I could swear something has run across my forearm. Then I shriek, drop the trunk lid, let go of the slippery quilts, bounce off the folding doors and have to start my search all over again.

I ordered the cordless light fixture that very day and in a couple of weeks a very small parcel arrived. I installed the batteries and pulled the string. At first I thought the fixture was broken but when I held it closer to my face I could see a glimmer of light. It's because of the bright sunlight, I told myself. It will make a big difference in the dark closet. It didn't make much difference. If I went into the closet, closed the door and turned on the light, I could be reasonably sure that I was the only large mammal present. The gloom was only marginally thinned and the difference between black velour and brown velvet remained elusive.

My order for the closet light must have put me on a lot of mailing lists because catalogues began to arrive addressed to me personally. Usually I resisted most of them but occasionally, curiosity or poor judgment prevailed. I gave the magnetic windshield cover to a brother-in-law who has to park his car outside. He probably never used it—the nasty little magnets were loose and would be impossible to control with a gloved hand. When our sons began making long winter drives in their small, defenceless looking car, I allowed maternal concern to prevail and bought "thermal insulation blankets, will contain body heat and save lives in sub-zero temperatures." They look like the fabric that those helium-filled birthday balloons are made out of, they weigh about half an ounce and they fold up to the size of a package of Jell-O. Mercifully the kids have never had to test the blankets.

The magnifying granny glasses that I bought to facilitate threading the sewing machine "really do work," I tell my husband. I don't mention that they work best when my nose is pressed against the free-arm on the machine and that by the time I look for them, remove my regular glasses, clean the grannys, replace my own and so on, I could probably have threaded the machine by feel and instinct.

We had a roll call at a Women's Institute meeting once that asked each person to show the most useless thing in her kitchen. One lady brought her "handy French fry maker, with stainless steel blades," so I know that other people succumb. Thank goodness no one I know has offered me a drink from a glass shaped like a human torso, and I don't think I know anyone who got their wedding rings from this catalogue—although the "Bliss Wedding Set" looks quite tasteful and the "Dazzling Celebration of Joy, Exuberance Wedding Set" would be worth something for the name alone.

By summer the catalogues were arriving at six-week intervals under threat of "Unless we get your order soon, this may be your last catalogue." Well, I didn't order, and the new issue arrived threatless, which says something about the company's integrity. Most of the items in the catalogue are remarkably resistible anyway. How about a "Christmas Toilet Seat Cover, in Jolly Red Felt" Jolly red felt would not wash well, and would one store it between seasons unwashed? Yuck! The "Glow Decorations" don't tempt me, nor does the "Jewellery Surprise Box," and even for the man who has everything I cannot imagine "Acupuncture Insoles." But wait—what's this? "Beautifully Decorate Your Tree With Unique Hand Painted Wooden Ornaments." I love wooden ornaments, and they look so cute in the illustration. Maybe just this one last time . . .

LEAVING THE House

WHEN THE PHONE RINGS in TV dramas, the lady answers, listens intently, fluffs her hair with one hand, picks up her purse and leaves the house. She steps into her immaculate car and speeds off to her assignation—legal, moral or otherwise. She doesn't even glance in a mirror, certainly she doesn't put on lipstick. Why would she? She's perfectly made up now. Any why wouldn't she be perfectly made up? She wasn't doing anything when the phone rang.

Oh maybe, once in a while, one of them wraps a bandana around her hair and vacuums a couch, and occasionally I've seen a woman dusting, but no one does anything messy. They never defrost the freezer, wash the bathroom ceiling or sort laundry into grubby heaps on the utility room floor. Of course they don't pick peas, process cauliflower, cut up chickens or let the macaroni boil over. They don't even cook anything that takes more than five minutes.

In real life a child phones from school having forgotten a book, or your husband needs a machine part or some grain tested. It's exciting things like this that send me scurrying from the house. But first I have to turn off the dishwasher, washer and dryer. I know they are all automatic, but I also know that the minute I leave the premises they will grin evil metallic grins and run over, spew out or start on fire. All right, none of them ever has, but someday they will, so I cannot leave the house with any of them running.

Often something is in the oven as well. Can I get back before it finishes baking? Should I just turn down the temperature, or shall I stall a few minutes and take the dish out slightly underdone?

And of course I have to change my clothes. Well I remember the time we got our signals crossed and the kid who was supposed to meet me at the principal's entrance did not. I had to go traipsing through the school wearing rubber boots and a faded dress with the hem trailing, and carrying a saxophone. I looked like a past-her-prime member of a punk rock group.

My hair will need brushing and I usually put on some lipstick. If there is any chance of a thunderstorm it's a good idea to unplug the TV and bring the laundry in off the line. Finally, I leave a note for anyone who might be looking for me and then I make sure the dog is out.

When I get outside and shut the door, I nearly always compulsively return to check that the oven and stove burners are all off, the sewing machine and iron are unplugged and my daughter hasn't left her curling iron on. Once I went to Sundre and left a batch of yogurt fermenting on a heating pad. I was sure I'd come home to a pile of ashes. I didn't, but I almost died of anxiety.

By the time I'm finally ready to go, I've usually forgotten my original reason for leaving. But that's all right—I always have time to think about it while I'm putting gas in the car.

COLD TERROR IN A *C*RINOLINE

WITH ALL THE WEDDING TALK lately I am reminded of the many weddings I have been party to. I have been bridesmaid several times, served as matron of honour, done the guest book, been the MC, given the toast to the bride and been the bride. I have memories from all of these weddings, some whimsical, some touching, some funny. I remember my own wedding very happily and I remember with cold terror the first time I was a bridesmaid.

The bride and I were not especially close friends, but my current boyfriend was best man and the four of us had been going out together. I was very young and totally ignorant of a bridesmaid's duties. My mother was perfectly bright and the bride's mother was a home-ec teacher so someone could have told me what I should be doing, but if they did I wasn't listening.

In any case I did not have a shower for her, I didn't help her shop for her trousseau or set up her apartment or write invitations, let alone choose china and silver. I was working in Olds at the time and she and all our families lived at Ponoka, so if there were any teas and showers they must have been held during the week and I didn't attend them.

I know now that in the weeks leading up to the wedding I was a poor excuse for a bridesmaid. But the worst was yet to come.

The wedding date was December 26, 1952, a date that is forever graven in my memory. The best man picked me up at my folks' house and took me and my bulky crinolines and blue nylon net dress to the Royal Hotel.

"I thought we would be dressing at Wilma's house," I said.

"No, no," Ted replied, "they have hired a dressing room here at the hotel. I reserved it myself, it's room 206."

Ted sped off to resume his best-man duties and I carried my finery through the lobby and upstairs. I found 206 easily enough, and was somewhat surprised to be the first arrival. I decided to change quickly and be out of the way when the rest of the party arrived. I peeled down to my slip and put on my crinolines and dress. The dress zipped up the back and I couldn't quite manage it. No problem—I would just wait a few minutes.

No one came.

There was no phone in the room, and I couldn't go downstairs half-zipped. I waited.

No one came.

I changed back into my other dress, I went downstairs and tried to phone, but the line was busy. I went back upstairs, I wept and paced the floor.

No one came!

I went downstairs again and tried to phone, but the line was busy. Now I was beyond weeping and was fast approaching throwing up. It was 1:56, the wedding was at 2:00. I tried to phone. No answer. I ran upstairs and put on my dress again, half-zipped. I would run to the church half-clothed, in high-heeled sandals, during a snowstorm. And finally here was Ted. He was so terribly, terribly sorry. The reception was being held in this hotel and this room was for the guests' coats.

We got to the church at 2:12. Everyone was looking very grim and the bride was pale green and shaking all over.

I lost track of that couple for years, but as their twenty-fifth anniversary approached I got their address from mutual friends and sent them a rather nice gift. They never acknowledged it.

PEA-PICKING PARTY
AND OTHER FESTIVALS

WHEN YOU LIVE on a family farm, you need all the help you can get. Occasional visitors might be asked: "Could you run out and dig a few potatoes?" "How are you at trimming hedges and cutting lawns?" "Would you mind watering those geraniums?" or "Can you please shut off the pump?" Regular visitors, like Ralph's brother Julien, really get into the hard stuff. He drives the grain truck, takes on major building and landscaping projects, builds and paints fences, plants trees, tiles bathrooms. He is more than a visitor, really. He is a godsend.

Our children grew up knowing that there is no "off-season" on the farm. Calving leads into spring work and gardening, which lead into spraying and haying, which lead into harvest and fall work, which lead into weaning and feeding, which lead to calving.

There were some breaks in there of course, like Christmas and perhaps a picnic, so in an effort to put a little more recreation in our schedule, we began to declare some farm holidays. For example, we have the Festival of the Calves, which falls in about mid-June and involves a lot of noise, mud and blood. The guest list for this is fairly large. My sister Donna and her family are often present, our son Mark has never missed it and our daughter-in-law Karen, daughter Kirsten and son-in-law Harry are usually here as well. For some reason the rest of the guest list changes from year to year. It has all the excitement of a Mexican fiesta without the mariachi band and the matador. The celebrants dress in their oldest clothes, and events include Creek Leaping, Calf Wrestling, Fence Climbing, Noise Tolerance tests and two or three other events that ladies may talk about but don't put in writing. Actually, since Ralph and I have begun using those little rubber rings, one of the more colourful events has been cancelled. This Festival ends with a barbecue and one or two angry cows tramping through the yard because their children were sorted into a different pasture than they were.

The Pea-Picking Party is a much more restful event. It can involve even the less athletic members of the family, and if conditions are right and a gentle breeze cools the covered porch, soft conversation and laughter prevails. Our children remember pea-shelling time as the occasions of some of the best conversations they had with their grandmas. I don't think Auntie Marie has ever missed a Pea-Picking Party. There are usually three or four to a season. Light refreshments are served.

Potato Planting used to be a big event, but with the kids all away from home we don't plant as many as we used to, so of course there are not as many to dig. Carrots are a big favourite in this family and we plant them with a seeder. We plant a lot and we use a lot, and that brings us to the Festival of the Carrots.

This festival is usually held on the last weekend in September and planned around the weather and the availability of a crew. First the carrots are hand dug, and then they are trimmed just below the crown so that they will not begin to grow in storage. The carrots are hauled by wheelbarrow to a clean lawn, where they are washed in warm water and spread to dry on the deck. When they are fully dried they are packed into plastic bags and put in storage.

While the outside crew is digging and washing, the inside crew is preparing a meal that consists of roast beef (no vegetarians in this family) and carrots, in various forms. Johnny Appleseed thought apples were versatile—well, they have nothing on carrots. Carrot soup begins the meal and it's delicious. Cooked carrots and rice are run through the blender and added to a milk base, following a recipe from Ralph's sister Alice. I make a carrot casserole that is so good that I have never taken it to a potluck without having at least two people ask for the recipe. It contains cheese and onion and Ritz crackers, and the recipe came from Bobbi Lentz. The golden glow salad has been made ahead from Lemon Jell-O, pineapple and grated carrots, recipe courtesy Auntie Georgia. Our daughter Kirsten makes the carrot pickles from a recipe we got from Nellie Davies. For dessert we have carrot pie from my mom's recipe, and we like it better than pumpkin. If the cooking crew has been really industrious there may be carrot cake for later, and occasionally we have carrot sticks and dip in place of the carrot soup. We haven't done carrot juice yet, but—one of these days. Steamed carrot pudding is not served at the festival. It is served only at Christmas.

Attendance has been falling off at these farm-based festivities. Do you suppose the participants have figured out that there is more work involved than there is recreation?

A MOOSE *L*EG IN THE FREEZER

NOT LONG AGO I dreamed that my mother and father were in Scotland. I had been there with them but I had come home early, I think for a rural child care meeting. Now Mom and Dad were due to fly home but they needed me to help them through customs, plane changes and crowded airports. It was 10:00 AM here and their plane left Scotland at 11:00 PM our time. I had thirteen hours to get there and get them packed and ready to leave. I didn't have airline reservations. As a further complication I had left my suitcase in Scotland and I didn't want Mom and Dad to have to cope with its contents— dozens of sweaters, towels, sheets, books and two shoeboxes full of old Avon bottles, some of which were leaking. I also was unsure where the suitcase was, as I have no sense of direction. I had left it in a hotel room but I didn't know the room number. I didn't even know the name of the hotel. I woke in a cold sweat, stumbled into the bathroom, clutched the edges of the medicine chest with shaking hands and stared into the mirror. My head ached, my chest hurt, and my eyelids were so puffy that they looked like they had been injected with Jell-O.

I have always had very vivid and usually stressful dreams. I can still remember the monsters that inhabited the nights of my childhood. There was the little man who went round and round the bed with a scimitar cutting off anything that hung over the edge, the magic troll that lurked in Mom's wardrobe and the green thing with long arms that snatched kids into the cellar or attic.

When our kids were small, my worst dreams were those that placed the kids in jeopardy. There were two main types of these dreams. In one it was a lovely sunny day and three little cherubs dabbled in a shallow bubbly stream, then suddenly a wall of white water and me screaming and grabbing and then jerked awake with the old puffy eyes and chest pains. In the other charming little scenario, the kids are looking out over a gorge or canyon when the ledge that they are standing on collapses. Either way it's too awful to be borne.

Until I was about forty I regularly dreamed that it was Sunday night and I hadn't done my homework. I also couldn't find some or all of my books and I had a massive report due on Monday morning. Sometimes this dream varies slightly—different problem, same horrible sick feeling. In one version I was extremely late for work at the Treasury Branch, I had lost my keys and couldn't remember the combination for the main vault.

A certain house appears in my dreams, one I've never seen in real life. It is a very old house with lots of very small, dark, low-ceilinged, poorly furnished rooms. Some of the rooms open off of a long hall. There are windows in the hall but they are small and covered with vines. Poison ivy, I think. Some of the rooms are in dormers and one gets the feeling that the dormers cling to the house only because of several layers of wallpaper. All the rooms smell damp and musty. There is something frightening about the house but I don't know what it is. Sometimes I am searching through a huge, damp multi-level basement that has dozens of arches, doors and hallways. Other quaint features include dripping pipes, puddles, cobwebs, grime and no washrooms.

Often a dream has some basis in reality. I'm worrying about my folks, we are planning a trip, I loaned Kirsten a suitcase. But one dream seems to be completely without foundation. In this flight of fancy I was expecting a big crowd for Sunday dinner. I went to the freezer to get a roast, opened the lid and found all the freezer contents bobbing about in three feet of water. A bag of marshmallows floated by and a whole chicken. A bright red tin of cookies added colour to the dreary mess. I couldn't stop to clean it up, I had company coming. I slammed the lid down. But wait, I still needed a roast. I opened the lid again and an entire moose leg bobbed to the surface.

I wonder if any book on dream analysis has a section on moose legs. I wonder if I need a psychiatrist?

HOW TO CLEAN
YOUR *H*OUSE IN TWO HOURS

I WAS WAITING in the checkout line at my local Co-op when a head-line on a magazine cover caught my attention: How to Clean Your Whole House in Only Two Hours. I snatched up the magazine. If you count things like closets, attics and the area under the deep-freeze, my whole house has probably never been clean all at one time. If this miracle was accomplishable in two hours I wanted to know how it was done.

Several days passed before I felt that the time was right for my two-hour journey into absolute cleanliness. I had my usual morning chores cleared away by 9:00 AM and planned to be finished with the cleaning by 11:00. Because I was unfamiliar with the routine, I felt I might possibly go over the two hours. This didn't bother me—even an extra half-hour of cleaning would give me time to fix a nice lunch for my husband.

Was preparation time part of the two hours, I wondered? The author used a minimum of equipment, I remembered. Obviously I was going to need the magazine with the instructions, but I couldn't find it. It was 9:20 when I thought to check my knitting basket and there was the magazine, folded open to an interesting sweater pattern. Aha! Well, now I could make up for lost time.

Right away I was disappointed if not surprised to find that this two-hour mission has absolutely nothing to do with closets, attics, under-the-deep-freeze or even ovens and refrigerators. Therefore, my whole house would not be clean in two hours. I had to accept this but felt that I had been seriously misled.

Now to assemble the cleaning materials: "upright vacuum cleaner, spray bottle of all-purpose cleaner, disposable dust cloths, lambswool duster with extension handle."

This was not an auspicious beginning. I have a built-in vacuum system, my cleaner is not in a spray bottle, I use worn-out T-shirts and towels for dust cloths and I don't have a lambswool duster even with a short handle. I compromised, but was already beginning to feel that the whole concept was slipping away from me.

"Start at the top and work down and forward. Begin with door frames, mouldings, picture frames, light fixtures and window frames."

I had chosen to begin in the utility room. We have an extra fridge there, and I thought the top of the fridge would be a logical place to start. No mention of fridge tops in the article, but what's a few extra moments? I began clearing it off—a large basket containing the kids' mail, a jar of water with ivy slips in it, my gardening gloves, some magazines I'm saving for my sister-in-law. Between the gloves and the ivy jar the area would need more than a casual dusting.

Guiltily I filled a pail with hot water and soap. Neither item was on the required list. The top of the deep-freeze could use a wipe while I was at it, and from there I progressed naturally to the fronts and tops of the washer and dryer and then back to the top of the fridge. My hand brushed against a miniature set of wind chimes and it tinkled cheerfully. I paused to examine it. It was so dusty that I was amazed that it could tinkle at all. I filled another pail with hot water and soap, took down the chimes and dropped them into the pail. Near the nail where the chimes hung perched a tiny dusty horseshoe. I dropped it into the pail as well. When it came to wiping door frames and mouldings, I was not actually following the article's instructions. They needed more than a wipe. I refreshed my soapy water and began washing the tops of the door frames.

The utility room leads to the entry, kitchen and a small hallway, which leads into the office and bathroom. Both sides of each of these door frames equals ten very dusty areas. Add the doors themselves and the utility room sink and floor, and my two hours were up. Nine rooms had never been touched.

I don't know why I buy these magazines. They never apply to me.

$\textbf{S}$KINNING THE HORSE

THE CHRISTMASES of my childhood tend to blur into a soft collage of snowy landscapes, fragrant decorated trees, wonderful food, Christmas concerts, mandarin oranges and family.

The Depression years were supposed to have ended before I was born, but there were seven of us and never enough money, so I know in my heart that our Christmases were quite simple. But there were presents and a tree, a lot of love, some squabbling and a wonderful dinner that began with a huge home-grown turkey. When the turkey came brown and crackling from the oven, Dad stroked knife to steel with such skill and speed that his hands blurred and the metals hummed.

There was dressing, gravy and whipped potatoes, turnips mashed with butter and brown sugar, home-canned corn, several kinds of pickles, homemade buns, cranberry jelly, and when you thought you couldn't eat another bite there was Mom's wonderful carrot pudding, with enough caramel sauce that you could, if you had room, be given an extra spoonful. From those long-ago Christmases a number of images come to my mind so clearly that I can almost smell and hear them: my brother Ronny hauling a too large tree into our small living room, Mom stirring fudge on a wood stove and laughing as Dad leaned in to inhale the chocolate–vanilla aroma, their early morning voices as they stuffed the bird, Mom knitting socks or hemming a dress in the light of a coal-oil lamp, Dad coming in on a gust of icy winter air and loading the kitchen table with bags and boxes of nuts and ribbon candy and mandarin oranges. Then was the Christmas that my older brothers made their first real money from their trucking business and filled the house with presents, and the Christmas dinner when my fork slipped off a pickled onion and shot it into Auntie Georgia's lap.

The Christmas that I was seven, my sister Marj gave me *The Princess and Curdie.* I read it again recently, and when I close my eyes I can almost smell it when it was new. If I keep my eyes shut and stay very still and quiet, all of us are in a sleigh on our way home from the Christmas concert. The rhythm of the horses' hooves, starlight so brilliant as to inspire awe, runners creaking in fresh snow, blankets bundled to our chins. Dad holds the reins and he is tall, strong and invincible. Mom cuddles the newest blanket-wrapped baby.

And then there was the Christmas that two-year-old Dale was so ill that Mom opened his presents early in case he was not with us for Christmas Day. He was, and still is. There was the Christmas that someone opened the cellar door and one of the cousins fell in. She lives on as well.

The worst Christmas was probably the one when Dad skinned the horse. Dad bought and sold horses. Our school ponies and our workhorses were like members of the family, but some horses came and went so quickly that we did not get attached to them. Fortunately the horse that died on Christmas morning was a "fox-meat" horse, so we were at least spared the weeping and mourning part of its demise. The only value in a dead fox-meat horse was in its hide and we could not afford to lose the money. While Mom banged pots, looked grim and issued tight-lipped orders, Dad skinned the horse. We ate a silent, non-festive dinner without him. It was early evening when I got dressed and went outside to see what was happening. By this time the hide was rolled and tied, and I tried to help haul it into the barn. Half a horse's weight must be in its hide—I couldn't budge it an inch.

Apart from the time that Dad skinned the horse, my memories of Christmas are warm and filled with love. Even that memory has some redeeming grace—"skinning the horse" has become a family code word for any activity that takes place at an inappropriate time. One Sunday morning, for reasons that are pointless to explore, I felt that I simply had to clean the fridge. Ralph came in from morning chores and found the counter covered in containers and his Sunday serenity seriously shattered, and he said very sweetly, "Skinning the horse, are we?"

One of the most valuable gifts that parents can give their children is good memories. When we remember our childhood as mostly happy and secure, then we tend to offer the same level of comfort to our children. May you and your family have happy memories, at Christmas and all year round.

MY CHRISTMAS LIST

IN OUR FAMILY we make a master Christmas list on one sheet of paper folded into sections. Everyone has a place on the list and everyone has access to it. You don't necessarily get everything on your list and you are not limited to giving only the items listed there, but the list is a great help.

I have saved our master lists for about twenty-five years and they are an interesting bit of family history. The kids' tastes and wants evolve from Tonka toys, doll clothes and Winnie the Pooh to chemistry sets and electric trains to computer equipment and designer jeans, and from rock to classical music, from toy pianos to T-Fal frying pans. Ralph's list has gone from extremely practical to less practical and occasional whimsy, and mine has remained about the same—books, records, candles. A couple of items have been on there for years.

This year I am going to do something different with my list. I don't expect I will get many of the things I am asking for, but I won't know if I don't try, and I have a lot of faith in the ingenuity of my loved ones. Some of these things are quite easily assembled or invented, and I'll bet there would be a big market for many of them.

I want a kit to carry in the car that contains a variety of stencils and a can of washable spray paint. When I pull into a parking lot and find that some fancy little sports car or some ancient clunker has parked right in the middle of the last two parking spots, I will leap out of my car, position one of my stencils and spray the following message on his trunk: THE DRIVER OF THIS CAR IS AN INCONSIDERATE SLOB. When I come back to my parked car and find that some ninny has parked so close to my rear bumper that it takes me ten minutes to manoeuvre free from my space, the stencilled message will say: BACK OFF, BONEHEAD. I haven't decided what the other stencils should say. Surprise me.

I want a kit that contains peel-and-stick labels in quite large sizes and felt pens in two or three colours. The kit should fit in my purse, so that when I go into a restaurant and a sign says BREAKFAST IN THE DINNING ROOM, I can quickly write DINING on one of my labels and paste it over the offending DINNING. I saw a sign at Christmastime that said STALKING STUFFERS. How I would have loved to whip out one of my labels and paste STOCKING on that sign.

I want a recording that I can activate with the push of a button when I see yet another travelling food salesman approaching my door. The recording will say: "Hi there, I realize that you are just a little guy trying to make a living, and while I sympathize with your situation and applaud your initiative, I am not going to buy anything from you. I must support my local businesses or they will fail. Your prices are high. My freezer is full. I don't have time to talk to you and besides that, we are thinking of becoming cannibals. Please go away and never return."

I want a portable lie detector so that I can say, "Stick your finger in this hole and then tell me that you mailed the cheque last week." I want volume buttons so that I can turn up people who mumble, and turn off bores and people who are foul mouthed and/or intolerant and hateful. I want there to be some way that the producer of a TV or radio program knows that I have turned it off. Maybe a light in the studio that grows steadily dimmer as people tune out.

I'd like peace, tolerance, honesty, love, food for the hungry, full employment, cures for all the major diseases and an end to crime and all the conditions that foster it.

I would also like the piano keyboard that has been on my list since 1988.

Embarrassing the Kids

ANYONE WHO HAS KIDS knows how it feels to be embarrassed.

One of ours told his grade two teacher that he had never tasted turkey. "At Christmas, my mom just cooks a big chicken." When I informed him that those big chickens were really turkeys, he was amazed and disappointed. He had expected turkey to be more exotic.

A favourite neighbour lady asked him, "Will you come sing for me when I get old?"

"But you're already old," he told her sweetly.

One of the boys told Grandma and Grandpa that the animals knelt over baby Jesus' crib to find out whether the baby was a boy or a girl. Two of them were hauling on a rack of books in Gray's Drugstore when the whole thing toppled over on them. And then there's behaving badly in public—breaking the neighbour's lawn mower or throwing up in a grocery store. Kids can be embarrassing. I knew that, I expected it, and I think we have taken these moments pretty well. What I wasn't prepared for was us embarrassing the kids.

For instance, I didn't know that after a certain age, no self-respecting kid goes grocery shopping with Mom. I didn't realize that when I accompanied them on a shopping trip, I must not say: "Those jeans are too tight," "Do you have anything less expensive?" or "What is this thing?"

Mothers should never call to a child when others can hear, and never address them by a pet name. If you have to give a child something in public, do it as unobtrusively as possible. Do not tell anyone cute stories about when your child was small.

I am not an especially mean mother, but now that I know the power of embarrassment, I am tempted occasionally to use it. I tell myself that it's for their own good—they shouldn't be so easily upset, they should toughen up and be less self-conscious.

From my long-time observation of parent-child dynamics, I offer these pointers for mothers who wish to toughen up their kids, or who just want simple revenge. These methods are guaranteed to drive your child bananas.

Weed public flower beds. Those big planter things at shopping centres are good—they stand at a convenient height and there are always weeds among the petunias. Find some lovely little junipers or Pfitzers that are choked with weeds, and liberate them while making angry remarks about slovenly maintenance and wastefulness.

Pick up someone else's garbage and put it in the receptacle.

Pinch a slip from a geranium in a park flower bed.

Allow yourself to be drawn into conversation with some odd character while waiting in a lineup.

Smile or wave at the nice elderly truck driver next to you in a traffic jam.

Fall against a locked door. I saw a lady do this at a school function recently. She tried to walk into a locked washroom, tried the next door and stumbled into the equipment closet. Boy, were her kids embarrassed.

This last one is pretty complicated. You will need new bifocals, three-inch clogs and a down escalator. With your children accompanying you, misjudge the bottom of the escalator, teeter foolishly for three or four steps, and fall onto your left knee and right shoulder.

It wasn't worth it. The kids were embarrassed, but they were concerned and sympathetic, too. I guess they are toughening up. They also laughed.

A LETTER FROM *A*UNT MABEL

IN MY COLLECTION of family memorabilia is a letter that my dad's
Aunt Mabel wrote to one of her great nephews. It's a two-page letter
composed of a single paragraph that leaps effortlessly from religion
and politics to travel plans and folk remedies, and twice she calls the
nephew by his brother's name. It's a delightful letter that conjures
up the image of a busy, bright and aware old lady who because of her
many interests has sort of ridden off in all directions. It's also a con-
fusing letter—one might say a "mixed-up letter"—but it's the PS that
makes it funny enough to be kept in the archives: "PS Jessie still
keeps writing that mixed up stuff. Last letter she said I didn't answer
her questions. I never said I would, I said I'd tell her what I think
about it. I hope she doesn't get poor Arlene mixed up."

Great Aunt Mabel has been dead for many years now, and when
she sat down to write this little mixed-up letter I'm sure she had no
idea that anyone but the recipient would ever see it. But here it is, a
permanent part of our family record, a link that we can touch, a bit of
her intellect and personality that brings a smile to relatives who were
not even born when it was written. How I wish we had something
written by her sister Ruby Anne, my grandma. We have not one
thing that was hers.

Many great books are compilations of personal letters. We have
Loving Letters from Ogden Nash and *Selected Letters of James
Thurber*. There are collections by F. Scott Fitzgerald, Winston
Churchill, Sir John A. Macdonald and others, all offering in-
sights into the writer's character and times that can be gained in no
other way.

You don't have to be famous to have your letters become treasured keepsakes. Wouldn't it be wonderful to have your great-grand-
father's letters to the parents he left behind in Ireland or Norway or
Russia? Wouldn't it be great to have even one letter in your great-
granddad's hand? Wouldn't it be lovely if you had one from your
grandmother?

Our daughter spent eighteen months in London and wrote wonderful letters home. Someday she will share them with her daughter and one day a great-granddaughter may read them and rediscover a grandma and a London lost to her otherwise. Our son lives in Boston and we have treasured and saved all of his letters for the same reasons.

I also have a collection of left-on-the-kitchen-table notes. Most of them are from the kids' childhood and all of them are priceless.

Dear Tooth Fairy,
My tooth is on the newel post where you need not risk hurting your feet on misplaced toys. I hope you will find this arrangement handy.
—Love John Olson

Dear Mother,
Ever since I supposedly spilled the glue you won't even talk to me for instance just now Mark asked you where you were going and you said, "to Nellie's" and I asked why and you just said "to get eggs" in a quiet sour voice. So if I don't talk to you for the rest of mine and your life you know why. —Kirsten

PS I love you even if you hate my guts.

MOM:
1—Lita phoned wanting you to judge safety something, (Speeches? essays?). 2—unidentified very quiet woman—sounded a little like Edna, a little like May. She will call back at supper time. (it was neither Edna nor May it just sounded like them) —John

Dear Kids,
The dryer is broken and Dad and I have run away to start new lives under assumed names. —Love and Good Luck, Art and Francine

A letter is a magical thing and its magic often intensifies with age. A letter is history and social comment in its most basic form.

Make some magic, make some history. Write a letter.

THE *B*EST CHRISTMAS PRESENT

ALL THROUGH THE FALL and winter I look for something special for my Christmas column, something that's seasonal, uplifting and happy. I want a story that's touching or inspiring. I want to find a little Christmas magic and share it. This is not easy, because while Christmas is prime time for magic and miracles it is also maximal time for songs and stories, and I sometimes think that every aspect of Christmas has been chronicled to the saturation point. How often have you heard, "Yes, Virginia, there is a Santa Claus"? How many stories have you heard about the Christmas pageant?

The roll call for our Women's Institute meeting one holiday season was "My best Christmas gift." Twenty-two of us were there and the answers were fairly wide ranging. I took notes.

Alice's then-boyfriend gave her a huge parcel in September that she was not to open till December. It was matching luggage, and forty years later it's still in use. Several people remembered unexpected and wonderful gifts during hard times—a Christmas tree, clothing, white furry boots, a toy piano. A lot of dolls were recalled fondly and of course children were terribly important. A son home for the holidays, a new baby, handmade gifts from grandchildren, gifts lovingly purchased with hoarded allowances, kids decorating each other in tinsel. The earliest Christmas mentioned was in 1918 in a post-war England that hadn't seen toys in years, and it featured Nellie's miraculous doll all dressed in blue silk by Grandma. More recent Christmases were Joan's family trip to Disneyland early in the New Year and M.J.'s happiness at being back home on the farm. Dorit remembered the magical moment when Nissen (Santa) appeared in her living room and a couple of guests remembered Christmases that signalled a long-awaited and blessed improvement in their health.

The truth is that there were about ten good stories and it will take me a good long time to use them up. Meanwhile, I choose to tell you Catharine's story about Duke.

Duke was a great big yellow and white dog. He was a collie of the classic Lassie type with a tapering head, erect ears that tipped forward at the ends and a thick, straight coat that formed a heavy white ruff about his neck and throat. His front legs were nicely feathered and his tail was a proud plume. He was beautiful and his personality matched his appearance. He was an adopted dog—the family got him from the SPCA. According to his papers he was about eighteen months old and had grown up in the city, but his barking bothered the neighbours and he needed a country home.

Duke loved his country home, and he loved the four kids aged five to fourteen who came with it. Across the road he discovered a charming lady collie and between them they produced several litters of sweet-natured roly-poly puppies. Duke had stumbled upon dog heaven and for several years he basked in his idyllic existence. And then, on a November afternoon, Duke disappeared.

Oh, the wailing and weeping, the searching and calling, the phone calls to the neighbours, ads in the paper, notices on bulletin boards. The fear that they would never find him and the fear that they would find him, his golden coat matted and bloody, his lithe collie body smashed by a car.

The desperate search continued for weeks, ranging farther each day, into coulees, under granaries. Had he been hit by a car and wandered off in a daze? Had he been stolen? Did the coyotes lure him off and kill him? A whole month elapsed. Prayers and letters to Santa made reference to Duke. It was all too awful and too sad.

Early Christmas morning, as the family gathered to open gifts, a sound at the back door attracted someone's attention. There on the doorstep, thin and bedraggled but very much alive was Duke. Can you imagine the celebration?

Duke lived on for many more years and never told anyone where he had been in the month he was away. Maybe he was following a star.

HAPPY *B*IRTHDAY TO ME

MY BIRTHDAY FALLS between Christmas and New Year's. It's an awful time for a birthday. Who wants birthday cake on top of fruitcake, carrot pudding, a million cookies, candy and nuts? It's an awful time for gifts too—by the 5th of January I have no idea what I got for Christmas and what for my birthday. Occasionally I get a largish Christmas gift and a note saying: "This covers your birthday too," and sometimes I get birthday cards tucked into Christmas cards. My birthday is a casualty of the season. It's nobody's fault, even I am unenthused about the occasion and a little embarrassed that it should fall at such an awkward time.

One year the kids decided that for my birthday they would make a special effort to brighten the day for poor old Mom. I was to choose the menu and they would prepare it. Anything I wanted, they said grandly. My wish was their command.

"In that case," I told them, "we will have a real change from turkey and ham. We will use that two-litre can of oysters that's been in the pantry for two years."

Silence filled the room.

"There are lots of things that can be done with oysters," I told them. "They can be made into a superb stew, a gourmet casserole or breaded and fried in butter. I think I will have them fried, and I will have rice, a green salad and sponge cake."

"Maybe you had better do the oysters," the chef said. "We will do the rest."

The instant that the can opener penetrated the tin I knew that we were in trouble. I don't know much about shellfish but I was reasonably sure that edible oysters smelled better than this. The nearest child began making gagging sounds. I ignored him and drained the liquid into the sink. There was a lot of liquid—in fact only about a cupful of greyish pulp remained. I gingerly picked up a shred of sludge and dropped it into the hot butter. The smell intensified.

By this time my daughter was kneeling on the kitchen floor, eyes cast heavenward and hands clasped beneath her chin. "Your prayers have been answered," I told her grimly. "Nobody is eating this mess. Go get some fish sticks from the freezer."

The table looked quite festive if you ignored the fish sticks. Uncle Jack had given us a bottle of wine at Christmas, and candlelight reflected in the wine glasses gave the room a holiday mood.

"Everything is lovely," I told my family. "What a pretty wine. I hope it's not one that I'm allergic to." I took a tentative sip.

Suddenly my face and neck were on fire and I knew that I looked like a case of third-degree sunburn. My nephew Lee leaned toward me and whispered conspiratorially, "I'm afraid it's one you're allergic to, Auntie."

"I will be fine," I told him. "It goes away soon." I made a "going away" motion and one of the boys, in an effort to spare my feelings snatched up the offending bottle. It slipped from his hand, bounced once on the table and spewed all over my husband's plate. Fish sticks floated onto the tablecloth, wine flowed into his lap.

"There won't be much on the rug," he assured us, "because both of my shoes are full."

During the memorable meal, the phone rang four times. I leapt to answer it each time because my mom and dad always phoned on my birthday and often some of my brothers and sisters as well. None of the calls had anything to do with the occasion. Two were about a meeting, one was a New Year's Eve invitation and one was a request for a punch recipe, although I have made maybe two punches in my life.

We older people took our coffee into the living room while the kids did the dishes.

"I'm glad that is over with," I said grimly. "What else could possibly go wrong with this wonderful evening?"

Six-year-old Kate appeared at my elbow. "I have to tell you something, Auntie Noreen."

"Go ahead, honey," I said, expecting some sweet little birthday sentiment.

"I'm very sorry," she confessed, "but I accidentally dropped your toothbrush in the toilet."

THE *S*AVING HABIT

I WAS PUTTING AWAY my birthday presents, and I said to the three kids, "Each of you lift a plant off the cedar chest and I'll put these towels away."

Now, if anyone should know exactly what's in the cedar chest, it is I, but even I find it interesting to dig in there on the rare occasions when it's open. The kids, tired of holding their assigned plants, set them here and there around the room and came to look over my shoulders.

"Good grief, Mother," my eldest said, "you've enough towels in there to open a steam bath. Why don't you use some of them?"

"The towel cupboard is full," I told him defensively. "As they wear out I'll replace them."

"As they wear out?" contributed number two son. "There are towels in that cupboard that you can read a newspaper through. How worn out do they have to be? And by the way, when did you last take anything out of the cedar chest? I only remember lifting plants while you put things in."

I thought about that for a minute. It's true—I can't remember ever taking anything out of the cedar chest. Anything that goes in there darn well stays there, including pillowcases and towels that were shower gifts twenty years ago. Obviously we've used some new towels and tea towels and things over that time, but they didn't go into service via the cedar chest.

"Look at these beautiful washcloths," my daughter said. "Can I take out a few right now?"

"Certainly not," I told her. "We have lots of washcloths in use. Save them till we need them."

"Mom," she said patiently, "we are the only people I know who have washcloths with little swimmer crests and half a waistband. The washcloth I used this morning was made from Auntie Donna's old towelling shorts."

My husband came to my defence. "She's improving. In our first years on the farm, she used towels worn right through in the middle. I used to put off coming in for meals, I hated those rotten towels so much."

"We didn't have much money then," I told them, "and you know I can't bear to throw out anything useful."

"We know," one of the boys groaned. "The only reason the attic doesn't cave in is because you have the downstairs closets packed to the ceiling."

I shut the cedar chest and started replacing the plants.

"Okay," my son said, "we'll use up the old towels. But at least hint to your relatives that we have lots of towels and we could use some sheets. The ones on my bed are shot."

I hope no one has any reason to check the blanket chest in our room—it's half full of new sheets. I'll give the kids some new sheets one of these days. It's just that the old ones always seem to have one more week's wear in them.

PREDICTIONS AND ᐯROPHECY

THE COMING OF A New Year traditionally unleashes a rash of pre-
diction and prophecy. Those who participate in this exercise fall
into many categories, including the semi-occult like Jeane Dixon,
the purely emotional like Louis Del Grande, pompous political pun-
dits, artificially enthusiastic sports personalities and a whole collection of totally unqualified amateurs whose predictions are general
enough to be harmless or innocuous enough to be easily forgotten.

As a representative of the latter category, I wish to offer the following predictions for the New Year.

In January I will once again resolve to catch up all outstanding
correspondence and do something about our twenty-five-year supply of unsorted snapshots. I will succeed with the correspondence
and fail miserably with the photos.

February will be grey and dreary with rotten reception on Chan-
nel 4, so that even if winter games venues are bare, there will be no
shortage of snow in our view of the events.

March will be made bearable by the arrival of baby calves and the
opportunity to pore over seed catalogues and start a few bedding
plants, which will either succumb to damping-off or freeze two days
after they are set out.

April will be full of growth. The first seeds will be planted outside, six million volunteer poppies will appear in the garden, the
mint patch that we tried to destroy with both Roundup and rototiller will have taken root in forty places and will threaten to swal-
low the farm, and we will find that the caraganas are still with us
despite our best efforts to eradicate them.

May will be its usual blur of field work, garden and yard duty. I
will buy more bedding plants than I planned on, and even after
every available space is filled I will buy six more flats because they
were on sale and needed water, and they would die if I didn't rescue
them. The three new cats we adopted last summer will all prove to

be female and we will have more kittens than we can handle. The hummingbirds will arrive on May 24 and we will welcome them as beloved friends returned from a perilous journey. And once again my husband will remind me that if I wanted a wedding anniversary that was celebrated with more than a passing note, I shouldn't have married a farmer in May.

In June our bone-headed dog will dig at least five crater-like holes in the flower beds before my screams and threats penetrate to his feeble memory bank and he realizes that he shouldn't do that.

In July we will not take holidays, not visit any parks, not go camping and not indulge in anything remotely resembling recreation. We may have a few meals in the gazebo, take a drive and have a few barbecues, depending on time and weather.

In August we will host the family picnic and, despite twenty years of practice and planning have four times too much food and forget to buy either paper plates or coffee. The hummingbirds will leave on August 25 and I will be stricken with end-of-summer blues and wish that I could go with them.

September and October will be devoted to gardening, gathering, preserving and preparing.

In November I will suddenly realize that the year is ending and that this is the time for handicrafts and Christmas baking, knitting and cross-stitch. I will make a last frantic effort to finish projects put aside for the summer and prepare for Christmas, family gatherings and the New Year.

I predict that the sun will rise and set 365 times and on about 300 of these days provide a spectacular technicolour extravaganza that most of us will be too busy, too preoccupied or too jaded to notice.

I predict that when the year comes to a close, most of my prayers will have been prayers of thanks, most of my fears unrealized and most of my worries groundless. Further, I predict that if given the choice of any home, friends or family in the world, I'd take the ones I have.

Happy New Year!

BRING ME A *B*OOK OF BEGINNINGS

WE HAVE A DICTIONARY of quotations, a rhyming dictionary and several of the regular kind. We have an encyclopedia, a Roget's thesaurus, two books of synonyms and antonyms and a couple of books of proverbs and epigrams. Some of these books are essential and all of them are helpful, but what I really need is a book of beginnings.

There is a proverb (which I can't find in any of my reference books) that says, in effect: "Well begun is half done." That is so true—the hardest part of any job is that first big step. Once you actually have the eggs separated, making the jelly roll is no big deal, in fact why not make three or four while you're in the business?

Lay out the fabric, decide on a pattern and the garment is half finished. Get all the boots out of the entry, sweep up the mud and grain and the actual floor washing goes quickly. Decide what's for supper, get the meat out of the freezer and the meal sort of shapes up on its own. Getting started is the hard part and that's why I need a book of beginnings.

The book of beginnings should be divided into several sections. It could start with some very basic advice, such as: get up, get moving, do something, and don't just stand there.

There could be a section on beginning a diet. Throw out all high-calorie foods, wrap masking tape around the fridge, cook only things you hate to eat and have someone take a picture of you standing beside a thin friend.

A section on beginning to prepare for dinner guests could advise readers to put away the sewing machine, take the ironing board out of the dining room and unload books and mending from the extra chairs.

There should be a whole section on writing letters and this divided into subsections. I need to know how to begin a letter to a twelve-year-old niece without sounding senile, and how to address my ninety-year-old Baptist aunt without sounding flippant. How do you start an apology? There has to be a nicer way than "Dear Zelda,

I'm sorry you overheard me refer to your husband as 'that pea-brained loudmouth.'" There should be a large list of alternatives to "How are you, we are fine" and "The weather here is nice." Brides would be grateful for a subsection on thank-you notes, which would advise them always to begin by mentioning the gift: "Your hand-tooled fish scaler is perfectly gorgeous and Fred and I will treasure it always." I am deeply resentful of thank-yous that say "Thank you for the gift," as if it were so mediocre that they can't recall what it was.

The section on beginning to write will also have to have subsections. The experts tell you to begin an article or feature story with a grabber: "City man fights grizzly," "Child finds diamond tiara." A work of fiction usually begins by establishing a mood and a central character. "Rain beat against the stagecoach windows, deepening Gwendolyn's sense of impending disaster." Variations of the classic fairy tale beginning "Once upon a time" are used more often than you would expect, and autobiographies are a cinch—they always begin, "I was born . . . " Straight news stories follow a formula: who, what, when, where, why. I don't know a formula for columns; I wish I did.

The most useful section of the book of beginnings may be how to begin breaking bad news. How do you tell your mother that you have smashed great-grandma's sugar bowl? How do you tell the kids that the old dog has gone to her final rest, or tell your husband that you forgot to turn off the pump and there was some funny blue smoke?

I hope someone writes a book of beginnings. Meanwhile I'm going to haul everything out from under the sink, then I'll have to scrub it out really well before I put things back. I've been meaning to begin that job for months.

Kittens in the Closet

FOR TWO YEARS our daughter Kirsten taught English in Japan. You collect a lot of stuff in two years and as Kirsten mailed things home, our spare room filled with boxes. She was coming home by way of Sri Lanka, England, Norway, New York, Boston, New Brunswick . . . and now she was on the phone with her latest itinerary and a small request. "Mom," she said, in a voice of sweet reason, "I can't leave her here, they treat their cats like, like, animals."

There was a fairly long and very expensive long-distance-to-Japan silence. "There must be someone you could give her to," I reasoned. "It's terribly expensive to ship her and she would have to stay in the house and you know how I feel about cats in the house."

"There is no one else I'd trust her to," Kirsten countered. "She is such a sweet little cat and it's only for a few weeks until I get home and get my own place."

So Spraglet, the little multicoloured Japanese cat with the Norwegian name that means "variegated" travelled from Japan to Ottawa and cleared customs with Kirsten's friend Joan and her cat, a male Japanese bobtail that had been "fixed" recently. Spraglet was indeed an affectionate, friendly, sweet little cat and she was also pregnant. Joan's bobtail had not been "fixed" soon enough.

As Spraglet neared her due date and became more and more rotund, she seemed to be looking for a dark, protected place. If we left a bedroom door open she was under the bed or exploring the recesses of the closet. Books from the lowest bookshelves began mysteriously to appear on the floor, and whenever I took out or put away towels, she would dart into the far reaches of the linen closet. A couple of times she explored the open dryer, and she showed a lot of interest in the spaces under the sinks. I put a towel in a big basket near her food dishes and she did curl up there occasionally, but you could tell that she was not entirely pleased with the arrangement. I took everything out of the bottommost shelf in the linen closet and fitted a box in there. I lined the box with old towels and showed Spraglet to her room. She popped in, turned around two or three times and purred. I propped the door open with a rock, and over the next few days I sometimes saw her going into or out of what Ralph referred to as "her office."

On Wednesday, Spraglet (or Nekko-chan—Japanese for "little cat") was uneasy and seemed to need a lot of attention. By evening she was uncomfortable and whiney but finally settled down and stretched full-length along Ralph's thigh, her needle-sharp front claws caught in his blue-jeaned knee. As long as he petted her, her eyes were tight shut and she purred softly. When he forgot to stroke her, the gleaming claws sunk a little deeper into the blue jeans.

On Thursday we had a very unhappy cat. She meowed almost non-stop, couldn't settle anywhere, was in and out of her office about fifty times, didn't eat, threw litter out of the box and all over the floor, sneaked past us and into the basement but didn't want to stay there and leapt into the lap of anyone who sat down. At about 4:00, when I sat on a stool at the kitchen counter, she jumped to a stool at the other end, ran along the counter and launched herself onto my chest. Her claws caught the neckband of my T-shirt and she pushed her head up under my chin, yowling all the way.

By 7:00 she couldn't settle for even a minute. I tried to hold her on my lap. When that didn't work I brought the bed out of her office and into the living room and tried to keep her in it, but she was so restless that she wouldn't stay anywhere. I wasn't about to let her have kittens on the rug, so as she moved around the house I followed with the birthing bed. At nine she made an awkward dash for the utility room, I followed her carrying the cat bed, and in a very few minutes she delivered, on the lino, a really homely white kitten with a short orange tail. It got cuter as she cleaned it. As soon as she had it nicely dry, she grasped it by the neck and ran off toward the linen closet. She got there before I did so Ralph had to haul her and the kitten out and hold them while I put the bed in place.

When we went to bed at 11:30, Spraglet and the kitten were very cozy in the linen closet. The Nekko-chan was purring, the kitten nursing. We spread newspapers all over the hall rug and hoped for the best. In the morning there were three kittens. The little white male and a vari-coloured female had bobtails like their father, and the second female was an almost black tabby with a long tail like her mom. There was no mess on the rug.

Spraglet was a very good new mother. She emerged occasionally to tell us what beautiful children she had and how good and smart they were. She ate and drank and returned to the babies. They nursed most of the time and grew like crazy. I don't know how to say "kitten" in Japanese but I guess Nekko-nekko-chan will probably do.

KITTENS *O*UT OF THE CLOSET

SPRAGLET AND THE KITTENS in the linen closet became the focal point of the house. Ralph and I sneaked peeks at them practically on the hour, and anyone who visited was immediately drawn to Spraglet's office to croon over the adorable babies. Three tiny bits of warm fur, eyes sealed shut, ears, toes and noses so delicate that they were almost transparent. They slept most of the time, cried in panic when they were lifted from their soft, warm nest and lay on one's open palm as helpless as protoplasm. At eight or nine days their eyes opened, and by the time they were two weeks old they peeked over the edge of their box in a state of perpetual amazement. Their faces were smaller and more triangular than those of Canadian cats, and the combination of huge, round eyes in a delicate face made them seem very wide-eyed and surprised. They were not really walking yet, but they were mobile within the confines of their box. Shaky little legs whose feet were fitted with minute pink claws reached, grasped and pulled the fat little earthbound body forward by a fraction of an inch. They crawled over each other with no regard for heads or tails, and when I looked in on the sleeping litter it was sometimes difficult to decide which limb belonged to which baby. Helpless and tiny as they were, they made their way to the mama's teats with a determined purpose that showed they were healthy and alert.

By three weeks, Spraglet began to take one of her children out of the box and play with it on the rug. Lying on her back, she would lift the kitten into the air and turn it round several times as if she were rehearsing for a juggling act. Then, using her front paws, she would clutch the kitten to her chest and practically lick its fur off.

By five weeks, the kittens were loose on the town. Still pretty bumbly and inclined to bump into and fall off things, they were all over the house but pretty well always on the floor. Kittens peered out from under the sofa and Ralph and I checked carefully before reclining in a chair or throwing a load of clothes in the washer. We watched TV with kittens climbing into our laps.

At six weeks they were everywhere. They used the litter box but they seemed to have contests to see who could throw litter the farthest. I was walking in gravel most of the time. The water dish was endlessly entertaining. A kitten would sneak up on it, dip a paw, inspect the wet paw while its eyes grew even larger, dip the paw again and walk off, leaving tiny wet tracks in the scattered gravel. The rungs of the chairs were just the right height for kitten gymnastics and they climbed and spun like acrobats in fur suits. They pulled the glasses cloth down from the handle of the fridge, climbed the towel that hung by the utility room sink and once, when I left our bedroom door open for a moment, they all got under our bed and into the box spring. One of the big chairs in the living room is covered and the kittens climbed up on it under the cover and became moving subsurface bumps. At night when I went to bed I closed my knitting or embroidery into the guest room. We placed large rocks around the bases of the dieffenbachia and schefflera because the kittens were playing in the earth in the pots. They batted brown ends into the leaves of the dracaena. They wrestled and pounced and leapt out upon each other from hiding. They knocked books out of lower shelves and jumped into cupboards and had to be retrieved. They were clean and cute and funny, they were full of joy and enthusiasm and boundless energy. They were endlessly interesting, and I, who never have enough time for all the things that I feel I must do, found myself just watching them and smiling.

We kept all the kittens until Kirsten came home, and for another week after that so that she could play with them. Then the white one with the short orange tail went to Joyce Mullen's granddaughter Karilea, the dark tabby with the long tail went to Kirsten's friend in Calgary, and the bobtail tortoise and white went to a family in Carstairs.

By the time Kirsten was established in her own home in Calgary, Spraglet had become a freedom-loving country cat and it seemed awfully mean to confine her to an apartment, so she is still with us. We love her dearly and her every wish is our command.

GARDEN *N*IGHTMARES AND DREAMS

LAST YEAR'S GARDEN was the worst we've ever had. The spring was dry and hot winds withered the apple blossoms so that they fell off without setting fruit. Our little Heyer #12 produced one apple, and the big crabapple trees bore only on the side protected from the wind.

The garden seeds lay among clods of hard, dry earth and germinated poorly or not at all. The thistles had no problem; they shoved mean, ugly shoots up from their network of underground roots and carpeted the garden in a dark green prickly layer. By the time the vegetables were high enough to see, the thistles were a foot tall and incredibly tough. The kids and I dug them out individually, and it was like uprooting small willow trees.

"This isn't worth it," I said, loading thistles into the wheelbarrow.

"Why do we do this?" I said, pulling a thorn from my finger that was so big and sharp it had penetrated my glove.

It began to rain. It rained and rained and it was cold. Hail fell six or seven times and the temperature dropped to zero. The radishes got wormy and went to seed; the beans were rusty and small; the corn was short and stubby, with nasty, tiny cobs; there were great gaps in the lettuce row.

"All this work for nothing," I said. "We should have summerfallowed the whole darn mess."

The sweet peas looked promising for a while—they were tall and bushy and full of buds. But the buds shrivelled up and fell off. The dahlias that I had started in the house and set out half-grown formed buds and sat and waited for sunshine; the portulacas drooped and became mouldy; the snapdragons snapped not.

"I've had it," I said. "Pour asphalt on it and make it into a tennis court."

On August 22 the garden froze hard. The poor baby pumpkins that had formed in rain were stillborn; the zucchini, which had never failed, finally did; the scrawny beans turned black; the early potatoes ripened off their tubers at the size of ping-pong balls; the peas formed big, fat pods that were empty.

"This is the end," I said. "Next year a few carrots, and enough onions and lettuce for a couple of salads."

At Christmas the weather was so warm and beautiful that the rich, black earth showed through in the garden, and on January 2 the first seed catalogue arrived in the mail.

Suddenly we remembered the smell and taste of fresh vegetables, and how green the lawn was, how beautiful the roses. The carrots had been really good last year, and the beets and cabbage were gorgeous. The frozen peas I bought on sale don't begin to compare with our own.

"I can hardly wait to start the garden," I said. "Is it too early to order some seeds?"

ACKNOWLEDGEMENTS

Thank you to Gene Hartman of Contemporary Graphics and the *Didsbury Review* for support and encouragement, for having cheerfully accepted every column just as I wrote it, for helping to publish my first books and for allowing me total freedom of subject and style. The only restriction I was ever given was, "Don't say anything libellous about an identifiable person or group."

Thank you to my family, who provide not only love and joy but constant inspiration.

Thanks to my agent Carolyn Swayze and editor Mary Schendlinger, who made the whole operation almost painless. Punctuation was never one of my strong points.

Special thanks to Will Ferguson. Without Will, this book would not exist. Without Will, I would never have submitted the manuscript to Douglas & McIntyre, and years from now I would be reading something and thinking wistfully, "Maybe I could have done that." I also want to thank Will for writing such a beautiful Foreword. I am overwhelmed. Thank you.